W9-DGI-699

THE TRAGEDIES OF
WILLIAM SHAKESPEARE

THE TRAGEDIES OF
WILLIAM
SHAKESPEARE

EDITED BY KATHLEEN KUIPER, SENIOR EDITOR, ARTS AND CULTURE

HUNTINGTON CITY TOWNSHIP
PUBLIC LIBRARY
255 WEST PARK DRIVE
HUNTINGTON, IN 46750

Britannica®
Educational Publishing

IN ASSOCIATION WITH

ROSEN
EDUCATIONAL SERVICES

Published in 2013 by Britannica Educational Publishing
(a trademark of Encyclopædia Britannica, Inc.)
in association with Rosen Educational Services, LLC
29 East 21st Street, New York, NY 10010.

Copyright © 2013 Encyclopædia Britannica, Inc. Britannica, Encyclopædia Britannica,
and the Thistle logo are registered trademarks of Encyclopædia Britannica, Inc. All
rights reserved.

Rosen Educational Services materials copyright © 2013 Rosen Educational Services, LLC.
All rights reserved.

Distributed exclusively by Rosen Educational Services.
For a listing of additional Britannica Educational Publishing titles, call toll free (800) 237-9932.

First Edition

Britannica Educational Publishing
J.E. Luebering: Senior Manager
Adam Augustyn: Assistant Manager
Marilyn L. Barton: Senior Coordinator, Production Control
Steven Bosco: Director, Editorial Technologies
Lisa S. Braucher: Senior Producer and Data Editor
Yvette Charboneau: Senior Copy Editor
Kathy Nakamura: Manager, Media Acquisition
Kathleen Kuiper: Senior Editor, Arts and Culture

Rosen Educational Services
Jeanne Nagle: Senior Editor
Nelson Sá: Art Director
Cindy Reiman: Photography Manager
Amy Feinberg: Photo Researcher
Brian Garvey: Designer and Cover Design
Introduction by J.E. Luebering

Library of Congress Cataloging-in-Publication Data

The tragedies of William Shakespeare/edited by Kathleen Kuiper.— 1st ed.
    p. cm.—(Shakespeare: his work and world)
"In association with Britannica Educational Publishing, Rosen Educational Services."
Includes bibliographical references and index.
ISBN 978-1-61530-927-6 (library binding)
1. Shakespeare, William, 1564-1616—Tragedies. I. Kuiper, Kathleen.
PR2983.T67 2013
822.3'3—dc23

                                                                    2012021217

Manufactured in the United States of America

On the cover: One of three prophesying witches revealing a bloody future for the title
character, played by actor Antony Byrne, in a London production of *Macbeth*, in 2007. *Elliott
Franks/WireImage/Getty Images*

Pages 1, 17, 26, 44, 82 Hulton Archive/Getty Images

Contents

Introduction	ix
Shakespeare and the Liberties	1
"We Will Play"	1
The Perception of Performance	2
Globe Theatre	4
The "Liberties" of London	6
Bearbaiting	7
City Playhouses	10
The View of Actors	12
The Popular Stage	14
Performance in Shakespeare's Theatre	17
Plays Within Plays	18
The Early Plays	19
Pyramus and Thisbe	20
The Internal Play in *Hamlet*	21
The Internal Play in *The Tempest*	23
Moral Regeneration Through Illusion	25
Tragedy in Shakespeare's Time	26
Elizabethan Tragedy	27
Christopher Marlowe and the First Christian Tragedy	30
Christopher Marlowe	31
Shakespearean Tragedy	34
From Comedy to Tragedy	35
The Fates	38
Shakespeare's Tragic Art	39
Decline in 17th-Century England	41

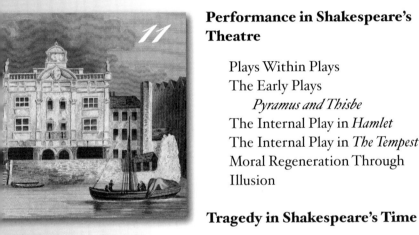

Inside the Plays: Shakespeare's Tragedies 44

    Revenge Tragedy 45
  The Early Tragedies 45
    Titus Andronicus 46
    Thomas Kyd 48
    Romeo and Juliet 50
    West Side Story 51
    Julius Caesar 52
    Julius Caesar the Man 53
  The Great Tragedies 54

    Hamlet 55
    Othello 59
    King Lear 62
    Hamartia 63
    Leir 66
    Macbeth 67
    Macbeth the Man 70
    Antony and Cleopatra 71
    Cleopatra Through the Ages 73
  Other Tragedies 74
    Timon of Athens 75
    Coriolanus 77
    Troilus and Cressida 79

Conclusion 82

Glossary 83

Bibliography 85

Index 87

LEAR. MACBETH.

RICHARD III.ᵈ HAMLET.

Mʳ GARRICK in Four of his Principal Tragic Characters.

149

Introduction

William Shakespeare's tragedies, such as *Hamlet*, *King Lear*, and *Macbeth*, are considered by many to be the greatest achievements in the history of the written word. That is not an honour lightly bestowed. Shakespeare's reputation as arguably the greatest writer of all time has been commonly accepted for centuries. Yet these tragedies are not simply esteemed because they are well-known products of a famous name that have gained exalted status through historical repetition. Rather, they represent the pinnacle of literary insight into most every facet of the human psyche. As detailed in the pages of this book, these plays continue to move and beguile both scholars and non-scholars to the present day.

The lasting iconic reputation of Shakespeare's tragic plays is primarily based on those works collectively known as the "great tragedies," a grouping of plays that typically consists of *Hamlet, Othello, King Lear, Macbeth*, and *Antony and Cleopatra*. But his tragic oeuvre is much larger and more varied than just those five dramas. His earliest tragedy, *Titus Andronicus*, was one of the first plays he ever composed and certainly the most grotesquely violent. An account of the betrayal of the titular Roman general, who brutally avenges the daughter raped and mutilated by his enemies, the surpassingly bloody work (by Shakespearean standards, at least) was in the spirit of the graphic melodramas that were popular in the late 16th century.

Composite showing actor David Garrick performing as the title character in three of William Shakespeare's great tragedies—King Lear, Macbeth, and Othello—as well as the history play Richard III. The Bridgeman Art Library/Getty Images

Another, and certainly more popular among contemporary readers, early tragedy is *Romeo and Juliet*. The story of teenaged lovers kept apart by circumstance has inspired countless other works of art over the centuries, from the beloved play (1957) and film (1961) *West Side Story* to the Disney television movie *High School Musical* (2006). While the play's major romantic plotline has been disseminated throughout Western culture to the point that the phrase "star-crossed lovers" is commonly known by most every literate adult, its additional explorations of family, loyalty, and honour remain enlightening.

Shakespeare's *Julius Caesar* straddles the definitional line between tragedy and history play. Like several of the tragedies, *Julius Caesar* is based on a historical individual and follows past events, circumstances that certainly would allow the play to be seen in the same light as Shakespeare's *Richard III* and *Henry V*. But it is the extent to which the character Julius Caesar becomes an "overburdened individual"—one of the hallmarks of tragic drama—over the course of the play that makes it better classed as a tragedy. Through the dramatic treachery of Caesar's close friend Brutus and the rest of the group that conspires against the Roman statesman, the play transcends the political concerns of the typical history play and enters into the realm of true tragedy.

Around the same time he produced his great tragedies, Shakespeare also wrote other works in the genre, but with relatively less success. ("Relative" because it is commonly accepted that even his "lesser" tragedies far transcend those that were produced from 1616—the year of Shakespeare's death—to the closing of all English theatres in 1642.) One of these so-called lesser works is *Timon of Athens*. Unlike most of Shakespeare's tragedies, the play has a fairly straightforward plot: The rich and generous Timon spends his fortune on others and is spurned when he is himself in need. He angrily leaves Athens and discovers more riches, which, in turn, brings back the attention of his former friends. The play ends with Timon cursing the Athenians and dying. The play is not one of Shakespeare's most popular efforts, not least because the nominal hero of the play, Timon, is a profoundly bitter and unsympathetic character.

Coriolanus is the last of Shakespeare's political tragedies. It is the story of a Roman warrior turned politician who is banished and then joins his former enemy Aufidius against Rome. As he nears the city, he is persuaded by his mother to spare Rome and is then killed by his new ally. The play is atypical by Shakespearean standards in that it has a single plot line and relies on understated dialogue or outright silence for its most trenchant moments.

Possibly the hardest Shakespearean play to categorize is *Troilus and Cressida*. Based on a Greek myth, the work centres on Cressida, a Trojan woman whose father has joined the Greeks, and her lover Troilus, son of the Trojan king. Like Romeo and Juliet, the two lovers are kept apart by circumstances beyond their control, as Cressida's father summons her to the Greek camp and she is forced by her situation to abandon Troilus and take up with a Greek officer, Diomedes. The rest of the play follows the principals of the Trojan War, presenting them all in an unflattering light. Typically grouped with the other difficult-to-classify works *All's Well That Ends Well* and *Measure for Measure* as the "problem" plays, *Troilus and Cressida* was placed in a category of its own by the editors of Shakespeare's first folio in 1623. The play contains many tragic elements, but cannot be considered an outright tragedy as most of the chief figures do not die and there is no tragic catharsis at play's end.

While there are substantial merits in all of Shakespeare's tragedies, the most insightful and moving are the five "great tragedies." The first of these, *Hamlet*, is also considered by many scholars to be Shakespeare's single greatest work. The play begins with the titular prince of Denmark being visited by the ghost of his recently deceased father. The ghost says that he was killed by Hamlet's uncle, Claudius, who has since married Hamlet's mother, Gertrude. Instead of acting immediately to avenge his father's death, Hamlet begins to behave as if he were mad in order to gain more information. A consequence of his plan is that he becomes (or possibly only appears, depending on one's interpretation) intensely indecisive, which gives rise to Hamlet's famed "To be or not to be" soliloquy. His actions, or lack thereof, cause the deaths of the courtier Polonius and his daughter Ophelia (who is also Hamlet's former lover) before Hamlet is able to enact his revenge and kill Claudius. Hamlet then dies at the hands of Polonius's son, Laertes. *Hamlet*'s psychological depth is what sets it apart from Shakespeare's other tragedies. The depiction of the troubled thoughts of the "melancholy Dane" is often cited as the most penetrating and multifaceted depiction of the human psyche in English literature.

Based on the Italian drama *De gli Hecatommithi* (1565), Shakespeare's *Othello* concerns the downfall of the play's title character as plotted by Iago, one of Western literature's greatest villains. After learning that Othello, a black general working for Venice, has appointed someone else to be his chief lieutenant, Iago convinces Othello that his younger Venetian wife, Desdemona, has begun an affair. Already concerned that his wife, at heart, would prefer someone closer to her own age and culture, Othello is overcome with jealousy and murders Desdemona. When Desdemona is revealed to have been completely faithful, a distraught Othello kills himself.

One of Shakespeare's most searing works is *King Lear.* The play begins with an aging Lear dividing his kingdom among his three daughters. The eldest two, Goneril and Regan, flatter their father and are rewarded while the youngest, Cordelia, refuses to be falsely obsequious and is disinherited. Soon, the newly empowered sisters turn on Lear and, growing increasingly mad, he is cast out to wander England alongside his loyal Fool. Eventually, Lear is reunited with his one faithful daughter when Cordelia and her new husband, the king of France, invade England to rescue him. Her army is defeated, however, and both Lear and Cordelia are captured. After other events lead to the ignoble deaths of Goneril and Regan, Cordelia is hanged; a broken Lear dies with the body of his one loving child in his arms.

The play's exceptionally downbeat final act speaks to the degree to which the gods are indifferent to the fortunes of most of its characters, if not completely absent from the world. A through-line of the play is the ability of some characters to turn away from the gods completely and instead find an inner moral strength as a means for triumphing over adversity. The evolving relationships of fathers with their children is another major theme of *King Lear*, as it is also explored in the play's moving subplot about the Earl of Gloucester, who spurns his one good son on the advice of his conniving bastard son. Gloucester is blinded and exiled by Regan's husband, but he is eventually found and nurtured before his death by his once-maligned son, Edgar, who, like Cordelia, has managed to find consolations against the evils of the world in an inner philosophy that cannot be affected by the Fates.

Shakespeare's *Macbeth* is the shortest of his tragedies, with no subplots to complement the main narrative. The result is a forceful story of the Scottish general Macbeth as he seizes power and is subsequently destroyed. The drama begins with Macbeth and his fellow general Banquo meeting three witches, who prophesy that Macbeth will eventually become king after first serving as thane of Cawdor and that Banquo will beget future kings. Macbeth is soon made thane of Cawdor, which makes him believe that the witches' prediction must come true. Accordingly, with encouragement from his wife, he kills King Duncan on the king's next visit to Macbeth's castle. Macbeth becomes king and then arranges the murder of Banquo to prevent potential future rivals to his throne. Lady Macbeth goes mad from guilt over her role in the murders and eventually dies herself, while Banquo's ghost haunts the power-mad Macbeth. The drama ends with Macbeth being killed by one of Duncan's sons in a manner that obliquely fits into the witches' prophecies, darkly fulfilling his destiny.

What sets *Macbeth* apart from the other Shakespearean tragedies is the degree to which the main character is responsible for his own downfall. Unlike the central figures in Shakespeare's other plays, whose ruin is precipitated by outside circumstances (such as betrayal by a friend or a loved one's murder), Macbeth himself is wholly responsible for his tragic end. Shakespeare paints Macbeth as a good-hearted individual who cannot deny his own ambition no matter the consequences. It is solely Macbeth's inability to deny his own inner demons that leads to both his brief triumph at obtaining the throne and his ultimate demise.

The final "great tragedy" is *Antony and Cleopatra*, which dramatizes the historical romance between Roman triumvir Mark Antony and Cleopatra, the queen of Egypt. Despite being in love with Cleopatra, Antony marries a countrywoman to heal a Roman political rift. However, his greater passion wins out and he returns to Cleopatra, bringing war with Rome in his wake. Antony is defeated, and false news of Cleopatra's death leads him to kill himself. Instead of being led back to Rome a conquered leader, a grieving Cleopatra elects to kill herself in the hope of achieving eternal life with Antony as lasting icons of heroic love, transcending the world that has brought the pair so much suffering.

No matter the setting or prevailing circumstance, each of Shakespeare's tragedies contains underpinnings of humankind dealing with the near-total abnegation of its agency in a remorseless reality that inevitably brings suffering to all that live in it. The emotions conjured by this perpetual losing battle are perhaps best, and most touchingly, conveyed in *King Lear* when the king grieves for Cordelia, his one loving daughter: "Why should a dog, a horse, a rat have life, / And thou no breath at all? / Thou'lt come no more / Never, never, never, never, never." The main actors in Shakespearean tragedy often pay the ultimate price—their lives—for their foolish choices or evil misdeeds, but their suffering is profoundly instructive to the audience. Further redemption for the tragic hero may be seen in each play's final scene, as the few remaining secondary characters are left to carry on, continually striving in much the same manner as the fallen hero. The persistence of hope as the ultimate, though apparently counterintuitive, antidote to remorseless and often random tragedy is poetically summed up in the famous words of the 20th-century Irish playwright Samuel Beckett, one of Shakespeare's spiritual dramatic successors: "I can't go on, I'll go on."

Chapter 1

SHAKESPEARE AND THE LIBERTIES

*I*n 1567 former grocer John Brayne went east of Aldgate to Stepney, where he erected a theatre called the Red Lion. It was the first permanent building designed expressly for dramatic performances to be constructed in Europe since late antiquity. The civic authorities of London, already unhappy with playing in the streets and innyards of the city proper, were not pleased with this new development. Within two years they were complaining about the "great multitudes of people" gathering in the "liberties and suburbs" of the city.

Illustration showing a Shakespearean play being performed in the yard of a London inn during the reign of Elizabeth I. Hulton Archive/ Getty Images

"WE WILL PLAY"

In 1576 Brayne's brother-in-law, James Burbage, joined the family enterprise by erecting The Theatre—a roofless, circular building with three galleries surrounding a yard—in the liberty of Shoreditch. Several companies performed at The Theatre, including Leicester's Men (1576–78), the Admiral's Men (1590–91), and Chamberlain's Men (1594–96). It was here that William Shakespeare would find his first theatrical home when he went to London, sometime in the 1580s.

The Theatre was joined by the Curtain in 1577. In subsequent years the liberties across the River Thames would also become sites of civic complaint as they became host to the Rose (1587), the Swan (c. 1595), and the Globe (1599), which was fashioned from timbers of the original Theatre. By the turn of the century, when the Fortune had completed the scene, the city was ringed with playhouses posted strategically just outside its jurisdiction. "Houses of purpose built...and that without the Liberties," as John Stockwood remarked in a sermon delivered at Paul's Cross (a public site outside and adjacent to St. Paul's Cathedral, and a major crossroads of the city) in 1578, "as who would say, 'There, let them say what they will say, we will play.'"

THE PERCEPTION OF PERFORMANCE

The drama of Shakespeare and his contemporaries is regarded by modern audiences as one of the supreme artistic achievements in literary history. In its own day, however, it was viewed by many as a scandal and an outrage—a hotly contested and controversial phenomenon that religious and civic authorities strenuously sought to outlaw. In 1572, in fact, players were defined as vagabonds—criminals subject to arrest, whipping, and branding unless

Engraving of the Swan Theatre (centre, flying flag) *and the surrounding environs of 1614 London.* The Bridgeman Art Library/Getty Images

they were "liveried" servants of an aristocratic household. Burbage's company and others used this loophole in the law to their advantage by persuading various lords to lend their names (and often little more) to the companies, which thus became the Lord Chamberlain's or the Lord Strange's Men.

Furthermore, "popular" drama, performed by professional acting companies for anyone who could afford

GLOBE THEATRE

Possibly the best-known theatre in the world, the Globe Theatre was built by two brothers, Richard and Cuthbert Burbage, who owned its predecessor, The Theatre. The latter had closed, ostensibly for good, in 1597, and the owner of the land on which it stood, in a London suburb, threatened to pull the building down once the lease had expired. The Burbages and their associates anticipated the threat, however, and in late 1598 or early 1599 dismantled The Theatre and carried the materials to Bankside (a district of Southwark stretching for about half a mile west of London Bridge on the south bank of the River Thames), where the Swan and the Rose theatres already stood. Eastward of these, they reassembled the timbers

Drawing of the original Globe Theatre, on the River Thames.
The Bridgeman Art Library/Getty Images

from the old theatre, calling the new building, which was probably completed by the autumn of 1599, the Globe.

Half the shares in the new theatre were kept by the Burbages. The rest were assigned equally to Shakespeare and other members of the Chamberlain's Men (the company of players who acted there), of which Richard Burbage was principal actor and of which Shakespeare had been a leading member since late 1594. The physical arrangement of the Globe was largely a matter of conjecture until the late 20th century. Although the theatre was known to have been broadly cylindrical in shape, with a thatched gallery roof, discovery of its foundations in 1989 demonstrated that it had 20 sides and was about 99 feet (30 metres) in outside diameter.

In 1613, during a performance of *Henry VIII*, the thatch of the Globe was accidentally set alight by a cannon, set off to mark the king's entrance onstage in a scene at Cardinal Wolsey's palace. The entire theatre was destroyed within the hour. By June 1614 it had been rebuilt, this time with a tiled gallery roof and a circular shape. It was pulled down in 1644, two years after the Puritans closed all theatres, to make way for tenement dwellings.

A reconstructed Globe—built using clues from a portion of the original foundation and referring to a number of extant Elizabethan buildings for hints regarding the structure, style, interior, and roofing—was completed in the mid-1990s and now stands near the site of the original.

the price of admission, was perceived as too vulgar in its appeal to be considered a form of art. Yet the animus of civic and religious authorities was rarely directed toward other forms of popular recreation, such as bearbaiting or the sword-fighting displays that the populace could see in open-air amphitheatres similar in construction to The Theatre and the Globe. The city regularly singled out the playhouses and regularly petitioned the court for permission to shut them down—permission that was granted only temporarily, most typically when such petitions coincided with an outbreak of plague. Elizabeth I liked to see well-written and well-rehearsed plays at court during Christmas festivities but was not inclined to pay for the development and maintenance of the requisite repertory companies herself. Her economy was inseparable from her political calculation in this instance, since the favour she showed the extramural playing companies served to keep the city of London—a powerful political entity on the doorstep of her own court—off-balance, properly subordinate to her own will and thus, as it were, in its place.

Attacks on professional popular drama were variously motivated and sometimes reveal more about the accuser than the accused, yet they should not be discounted too readily, for they have a great deal to communicate about the cultural and historical terrain that Shakespeare's theatre occupied in its own day. Nowhere is this more the case than in one of the most consistent focal points of outrage, sounded regularly from the pulpit and in lord mayors' petitions, toward these "Houses of purpose built...and that without the Liberties"—the place of the stage itself.

THE "LIBERTIES" OF LONDON

The "liberties or suburbs" of early modern London bear little resemblance to modern suburbs in either a legal or a cultural sense. They were a part of the city, extending up to 3 miles (5 kilometers) from its ancient Roman wall, yet in crucial aspects were set apart from it. They were also an integral part of a complex civic structure common to the walled medieval and Renaissance metropolis, a marginal geopolitical domain that was nonetheless central to the symbolic and material economy of the city. Free, or "at

BEARBAITING

A popular entertainment, bearbaiting involved the setting of dogs on a bear—or, in the case of bullbaiting, a bull—chained to a stake by the neck or leg. Prevalent in England from the 12th to the 19th century, when they were banned as inhumane, these spectacles were usually staged at theatre-like arenas known as bear gardens.

In England many large groups of bears were kept expressly for the purpose. Contemporary records reveal, for example, that 13 bears were provided for an entertainment attended by Queen Elizabeth I in 1575.

When a bull was baited, its nose was often blown full of pepper to further arouse it. Specially trained dogs were loosed singly, each attempting to seize the tethered animal's nose. Often a hole in the ground was provided for the bull to protect its snout. A successful dog was said to have pinned the bull.

Variations on these activities included whipping a blinded bear and baiting a pony with an ape tied to its back. Dogfighting and cockfighting were often provided as companion diversions.

Bearbaiting and bullbaiting and the variations on these "sports" began to decline in popularity, although very slowly, from the late 17th century onward. They were permanently outlawed by act of Parliament in England in 1835, by which time they had also been outlawed in most countries in northern Europe.

liberty," from manorial rule or obligations to the crown, the liberties "belonged" to the city yet fell outside the jurisdiction of the lord mayor, the sheriffs of London, and the Common Council. They constituted an ambiguous geopolitical domain over which the city had authority but, paradoxically, almost no control. Liberties existed inside the city walls as well—it was in them that the so-called private, or hall, playhouses were to be found—but they too stood "outside" the city's effective domain. Whatever their location, the liberties formed an equivocal territory that was at once internal and external to the city, neither contained by civic authority nor fully removed from it.

Clearly, the freedom from London's legal jurisdiction was crucial to the survival of the playhouses in a pragmatic sense, but the city's outrage and sense of scandal cannot be fully explained by jurisdictional frustration alone. The liberties had for centuries performed a necessary cultural and ideological function in the city's symbolic economy, one that can be only briefly summarized here but that made them peculiarly apt ground for early modern drama to appropriate and turn to its own use and livelihood. Early modern cities were shaped, their common spaces inscribed with communal meaning and significance, by a wide variety of ritual, spectacle, and customary pastimes. Inside the city walls, ritual traditions were organized around central figures of authority, emblems of cultural coherence. The marginal traditions of the liberties, by contrast, were organized around emblems of anomaly and ambivalence. Whatever could not be contained within the strict order of the community, or exceeded its bounds in a symbolic or moral sense, resided there, and it was a strikingly heterogeneous zone.

In close proximity to brothels and hospitals stood monasteries—markers, in a sense, of the space between this life and the next—until such church holdings were seized by the crown following Henry VIII's break with Rome. Gaming houses, taverns, and bearbaiting arenas nestled beside sites for public execution, marketplaces, and, at the extreme verge of the liberties, the city's leprosariums. Viewed from a religious perspective, the liberties were marked as places of the sacred, or of sacred pollution

Woodcut image from "A Book of Roxburghe Ballads"—a collection of broadsides featuring the lyrics of popular ballads—showing an Elizabethan street scene. Private Collection/The Bridgeman Art Library

in the case of the city's lepers, made at once holy and hopelessly contaminated by their affliction. From a political perspective, the liberties were the places where criminals were conveyed for public executions, well-attended and sometimes festive rituals that served to mark the boundary between this life and the next in a more secular fashion. From a general point of view, the margins of the city were places where forms of moral excess such as prostitution were granted license to exist beyond the bounds of a community that they had, by their incontinence, already exceeded.

This civic and social structure had been remarkably stable for centuries, primarily because it made room for what it could not contain. As the population of London underwent an explosive expansion in the 16th century, however, the structure could no longer hold, and the reigning hierarchy of London found the spectacle of its own limits thrust upon it. The dissolution of the monasteries had made real estate in the liberties available for private enterprises. The traditional sanctuary and freedom of the city's margins were thus opened to new individuals and social practices. Victims of enclosure, masterless men, foreign tradesmen without guild credentials, outlaws, and prostitutes joined radical Puritans and players in taking over and putting the liberties to their own uses, but it was the players who had the audacity to found a viable and highly visible institution of their own on the grounds of the city's well-maintained contradictions. And it was the players too who converted the traditional liberty of the suburbs into their own dramatic license, establishing a liberty that was at once moral, ideological, and topological—a "liberty" that gave the stage an impressive freedom to experiment with a wide range of perspectives on its own times.

CITY PLAYHOUSES

Playhouses also existed within the city walls, but they operated on a more limited scale. Acting companies composed entirely of young boys performed sporadically in the city's intramural liberties from 1576 to 1608, until repeated offenses to the crown provoked James I to disband all boys' companies. After 1608 at Blackfriars, Whitefriars, and other hall playhouses, adult companies from the extramural liberties moved into the city as well and regularly performed in both the hall and the arena playhouses.

The boys' repertory was a highly specialized one: more than 85 percent of their dramatic offerings were comedies, largely satirical—a genre that was conversely rare on the arena stages. The difference is a significant one. Although satire frequently outraged its specific targets, its immediate topicality also limited its ideological

Engraving of the Dorset Garden Theatre, which was accessible by boat. Although this theatre did not open until 1671, it is similar to the hall playhouses operating in London during Shakespeare's lifetime.
Science & Society Picture Library/Getty Images

range and its capacity to explore broad cultural issues. As dramatic genres, city comedy and satire were relatively contained forms of social criticism. In terms of repertory as well as topology, the hall playhouses produced what might be called an "interstitial" form of drama, one that was lodged, like the theatres themselves, in the gaps and seams of the social fabric.

In contrast to the hall theatres, the open-air playhouses outside the city walls evolved what Nicholas Woodrofe, lord mayor of London in 1580, regarded as an "incontinent" form of drama:

> Some things have double the ill, both naturally
> in spreading the infection, and otherwise in

drawing God's wrath and plague upon us, as the erecting and frequenting of houses very famous for incontinent rule out of our liberties and jurisdiction.

THE VIEW OF ACTORS

Playhouses were regarded not merely as a breeding ground for the plague but as the thing itself, an infection "pestering the City" and contaminating the morals of London's apprentices. Theatres were viewed as houses of Proteus, and, in the metamorphic fears of the city, it was not only the players who shifted shapes, confounded categories, and counterfeited roles. Drama offered a form of "recreation" that drew out socially unsettling reverberations of the term, since playhouses offered a place "for all masterless men and vagabond persons that haunt the highways, to meet together and *to recreate themselves* [emphasis added]." The fear was not that the spectators might be entertained but that they might incorporate theatrical means of impersonation and representation in their own lives—for example, by dressing beyond their station and thus confounding a social order reliant on sumptuary codes to distinguish one social rank from another.

What the city objected to was the sheer existence of the playhouses and the social consequences of any form of theatricality accessible to such a broad spectrum of the population. In contrast, religious antitheatricality, whether Anglican or Puritan, extended to issues of content and the specific means of theatrical representation employed by acting companies. Puritans were particularly incensed by the transvestite character of all English companies prior to the Restoration. Women onstage would have outraged them as well, but the practice of having boys don women's apparel to play female roles provoked a host of irate charges. Such cross-dressing was viewed by Puritans as a violation of biblical strictures that went far beyond issues of costuming. On the one hand, it was seen as a substantive transgression of gender boundaries. The adoption of women's dress contaminated, or "adulterated," one's gender, producing a hybrid and effeminate man. On the other hand, transvestite acting was assumed to excite a sodomitic erotic desire in the audience, so that after the play "everyone brings

Photograph of a young actor playing the female lead character in Shakespeare's Troillus and Cressida *in Edinburgh, Scotland, 1958. In Elizabethan England, female characters traditionally were played by boys.* John Pratt/Hulton Archive/Getty Images

another homeward of their way very friendly and in their secret enclaves they play sodomite or worse."

Puritan charges tend to the rather imaginative, to say the least. They do serve as a reminder, however, that the transvestite tradition in English acting was not without controversy. Until the late 20th century, critics tended to explain it away, ascribing its origins to biblical prohibitions about women's public behaviour and regarding its significance as minimal, except when a particular play (such as *As You Like It*) made thematic use of cross-dressing. Otherwise (so the argument went), it was a convention that the audience was trained not to perceive. Boys were taken for women onstage and learned their craft by first serving such an apprenticeship. It now appears that male sexual practice in Renaissance England was often bisexual rather than strictly heterosexual and that sexual relations between males typically involved a disparity in age. In relations with the same as with the opposite sex, the sexual relationship was also a power relationship based on hierarchy and dominance by the (older) male. It is quite possible that boy actors were also the sexual partners of the adult actors in the company. When such boys played women, their fictive roles reproduced their social reality in terms of sexual status and subordination. To what degree the audience responded to the actor, the character portrayed, or an erotically charged hybrid of the two is impossible to say, but, as the Shakespeare scholar Stephen Orgel has noted, transvestite actors must have appealed to both men and women, given the large number of the latter who attended the theatre.

THE POPULAR STAGE

The drama that developed in the arena playhouses of early modern London was rich in its diversity, aesthetically

An artist's rendering of theatregoers enjoying a show at the original Globe. Popular theatre was accessible to the general public and was capable of informing as well as entertaining the masses. Time & Life Pictures/Getty Images

complex, and ideologically powerful in its far-reaching cultural and political resonance. And literacy was not the price of admission to Shakespeare's theatre. Consequently, the popular stage enjoyed a currency and accessibility that was rivaled only by the pulpit and threatened to eclipse it. Elizabethan and Jacobean drama is not normally thought of primarily in terms of the information it disseminated, but it gave the illiterate among its audience unprecedented access to ideas and ideologies, stories fictive and historical, all affectively embodied and drawn from an impressive repertoire that ranged from the classical to the contemporary. In doing so, the Renaissance stage combined with other forces (such as the rapid expansion of print culture and what is believed to have been a slow but steady rise in literacy) to alter the structure of knowledge by redefining and expanding its boundaries.

Born of the contradiction between court license and civic prohibition, popular theatre emerged as a viable cultural institution only by materially embodying this contradiction, dislocating itself from the strict confines of the social order and taking up a place on its margins. From this vantage point, as contemporaneous fears and modern audiences' continuing fascination testify, the popular stage developed a remarkable capacity to explore and realize, in dramatic form, some of the fundamental controversies of its time. In effect, the stage translated London's social and civic margins, the liberties of the city, into margins in the textual sense: into places reserved for a "variety of senses" (as the translators of the 1611 Bible described their own margins) and for divergent points of view—for commentary upon and even contradiction of the main body of their text, which in this instance means the body politic itself.

Chapter 2

PERFORMANCE IN SHAKESPEARE'S THEATRE

A hundred yards or so southeast of the new Globe Theatre is a vacant lot surrounded by a corrugated-iron fence marked with a bronze plaque as the site of the original Globe Theatre of 1599. A little closer to the new Globe, one can peer through dirty slit windows into a dimly lit space in the basement of a new office building, next to London Bridge, where about two-thirds of the foundations of the Elizabethan Rose Theatre can barely be made out. A little farther to the west, the new Globe rises up on the Bankside, asserting definite knowledge of William Shakespeare's theatre and deserving praise for doing so. But the difficulty of seeing the earlier theatres in the shadows of the past better represents our understanding of performance in Shakespeare's theatre.

Acting style—realistic or melodramatic—stage settings, props and machinery, swordplay, costumes, the speed with which the lines were delivered, length of performance, entrances and exits, boys playing the female roles, and other performance details remain problematic. Even the audience—rowdy, middle-class, or intellectual—is difficult to see clearly. Scholars have determined something of the mise-en-scène, but not nearly enough. While the historians continue their painstaking researches, the best general sense of Shakespeare in his theatre still comes from the little plays within his plays that across the centuries still give us something of the feel of performance in the Elizabethan theatre.

PLAYS WITHIN PLAYS

The internal play appears frequently in the early plays *The Taming of the Shrew*, *Love's Labour's Lost*, and *A Midsummer Night's Dream*. *The Taming of the Shrew*, for example, is a theatrical tour de force, consisting of plays set within plays and actors watching other actors acting, seemingly extending into infinity. All the world is a stage in Padua, where the theatre is the true image of life. In the outermost frame-play, the drunken tinker Christopher Sly is picked out of the mud by a rich lord and transported to his house. A little pretense is arranged, purely for amusement,

A scene from The Taming of the Shrew, *wherein Christopher Sly awakens to find himself treated like a lord. Sly's story is the framing conceit around which the play's action takes place although it is sometimes eliminated in performance.* Universal Images Group/ Getty Images

and when Sly awakes he finds himself in rich surround-ings, addressed as a nobleman, obeyed in every wish, and waited on by a beautiful wife. At this point professional players appear, to provide entertainment. They are warmly welcomed and fed, and then they put on a play before Sly about the taming of Kate the shrew.

Shakespeare records the problems of playing and of audiences in more detail in *A Midsummer Night's Dream*. No players could be more hopeless than Nick Bottom, the weaver, and his amateur friends, who, in the hope of win-ning a small pension, perform the internal play, *Pyramus and Thisbe*, to celebrate the triple marriage of Duke Theseus and two of his courtiers. Bottom's company is so literal-minded as to require that the moon actu-ally shine, that the wall through which Pyramus and Thisbe speak be solidly there, and that the actor who plays the lion assure the ladies in the audience that he is only a make-believe lion. The literalness which lies behind such a materialistic conception of theatre is at odds with Shakespeare's poetic drama that created most of its illusion with words, rich costumes, and a few props. In other respects too, the actors' stumbling rant, missed cues, mispronounced words and lines, willingness to converse directly with the audience, doggerel verse, and general ineptitude constitute a playwright's nightmare of dramatic illusion trampled into nonsense.

THE EARLY PLAYS

The courtly audience at *Pyramus and Thisbe* is socially superior to the actors but little more sophisticated about what makes a play work. The duke does under-stand that, though this play may be, as his betrothed Hippolyta says, "the silliest stuff" he ever heard, it lies

PYRAMUS AND THISBE

One of the broadest internal plays of Shakespeare, that of *Pyramus and Thisbe*, occurs in *A Midsummer Night's Dream*. The originals of the narrative enacted there were the hero and heroine of a Babylonian love story, who were able to communicate with each other only through a crack in the wall between their houses. The tale was related by Roman poet Ovid (43 BCE–17 CE) in his *Metamorphoses, Book IV*. Though their parents refused to consent to their union, the lovers at last resolved to flee together and agreed to meet under a mulberry tree. Thisbe, first to arrive, was terrified by the roar of a lioness and took to flight. In her haste she dropped her veil, which the lioness tore to pieces with jaws stained with the blood of an ox. Pyramus, believing that Thisbe had been devoured by the lioness, stabbed himself. When Thisbe returned and found her lover mortally wounded under the mulberry tree, she put an end to her own life. From that time forward, legend relates, the fruit of the mulberry, previously white, appeared reddish-black.

The story was told in Geoffrey Chaucer's 14th-century dream vision *Legend of Good Women* before it was made farcical by Shakespeare's "rude mechanicals." Some readers will also detect echos of its outline in Shakespeare's *Romeo and Juliet*.

within the power of a gracious audience to improve it, for the best of actors "are but shadows; and the worst are no worse, if imagination amend them." But the nobles in the audience have little of the necessary audience imagination. They mock the actors and talk loudly among themselves during the performance. They are as literal-minded in their own way as the actors, and, as if unaware that they too are actors sitting on a stage, they laugh at what unrealistic and trivial things all plays and players are.

The necessity for "symbolic performance," which is indirectly defended in these early plays by showing a too-realistic opposite, is explained and directly apologized for in *Henry V*, written about 1599, where a Chorus speaks for the "bending author" and his actors who "force a play" on the "unworthy scaffold," the stage of the Globe's "wooden O." Here "time...numbers, and due course of things, /... cannot in their huge and proper life / Be...presented" by players and a playwright who unavoidably must "in little room [confine] mighty men."

THE INTERNAL PLAY IN *HAMLET*

It is through one of his tragedies, however, that Shakespeare offers his most detailed image of theatrical performance. In *Hamlet* a professional repertory troupe, similar to Shakespeare's own Chamberlain's Men, comes to Elsinore and performs *The Murder of Gonzago* before the Danish court. Once arrived at the Danish palace, the players are servants, and their low social status determines their treatment by the king's councillor, Polonius. However, Hamlet greets them warmly: "You are welcome, masters; welcome, all. I am glad to see thee well. Welcome, good friends." He jokes familiarly with the boy who plays female parts about his voice deepening, which will end his ability to play these roles, and twits one of the younger players about his new beard: "O, old friend! Why, thy face is valanced since I saw thee last. Com'st thou to beard me in Denmark?" Hamlet is a theatre buff, like one of the young lords or lawyers from the Inns of Court who sat on the stage or in the gallery boxes above the stage in the London theatres and commented loudly and wittily on the action. Like them, too, he knows the latest neoclassical aesthetic standards and looks down on what he considers the crudity of the popular theatre: its ranting tragedians, melodramatic acting styles, parts "to tear a cat in," bombastic blank verse, "inexplicable dumb shows," vulgar clowns who improvise too much, and the crude audience of "groundlings" who watch the play from the pit. The prince has elevated views of acting—"Suit the action to the word, the word to the action,...o'erstep not the modesty of nature"—and of play construction—"well digested in the scenes, set down with as much modesty as cunning."

The players fail to meet Hamlet's neoclassical standards in both their acting style and their plays. *The Murder of Gonzago* is an old-fashioned, rhetorical, bombastic tragedy, structured like a morality play, beginning with a dumb show and filled with stiff formal speeches. But the play does "hold as 'twere the mirror up to nature, to show virtue her feature, scorn her own image, and the very age and body of the time his form and pressure." *The Murder of Gonzago*, for

Illustration depicting the traveling players in Hamlet *staging* The Murder of Gonzago, *the performance of which the young prince hopes will "catch the conscience of the king."* Kean Collection/ Archive Photos/ Getty Images

all its artistic crudity, reveals the hidden disease of Denmark, the murder of the old king by his brother.

But the effect on the audience of this theatrical truth is not what either Hamlet or Shakespeare might hope for. Gertrude fails to see, or ignores, the mirror of her own unfaithfulness held up to her by the player queen: "The lady doth protest too much, methinks." Claudius, realizing his crime is known, immediately plots to murder Hamlet. Even Hamlet the critic is a bad audience. During the performance he makes loud remarks to other members of the audience, baits the actors, criticizes the play, and misses its main point about the necessity of accepting the imperfections of the world and of oneself.

THE INTERNAL PLAY IN *THE TEMPEST*

Performance in these internal plays is always unsatisfactory in some respect, and the audience must for the most part read Shakespeare's own views on theatrical matters in reverse of these mirror stages. Only near the end of his career does Shakespeare present an idealized theatre of absolute illusion, perfect actors, and a receptive audience. In *The Tempest* (*c.* 1611), Prospero, living on a mysterious ocean island, is a magician whose art consists of staging redemptive illusions: storm and shipwreck, an allegorical banquet, "living drolleries," a marriage masque, moral tableaux, mysterious songs, and emblematic set pieces. All of these "playlets" have for once the desired effect on most of their audiences, bringing them to an admission of former crimes, repentance, and forgiveness. In Ariel, the spirit of fancy and playfulness, and his "rabble" of "meaner fellows," the playwright at last finds perfect actors who execute his commands

Illustration from an 1850s edition of The Tempest, *showing the sprite Ariel taking the form of a harpy. Scholars have likened Ariel's shape-shifting to an actor's ability to transform into a character.* Universal Images Group/Getty Images

with lightning swiftness, taking any shape desired in an instant. Prospero's greatest play is his "masque of Juno and Ceres," which he stages as an engagement celebration for his daughter and Prince Ferdinand. The masque tells the young lovers of the endless variety, energy, and fruitfulness of the world and reassures them that these things will be theirs to enjoy in their marriage.

But Shakespeare's old doubts about plays, theatres, players, and audiences still are not silenced. Prospero's masque is broken off by a crowd of drunken rowdies, and he, like some medieval poet writing his palinode, abjures his "rough magic," breaks and buries his staff, and drowns his book "deeper than did ever plummet sound." The great masque is spoken of slightingly only as "some vanity of mine art," and, when the performance is over, the actors and the play, however extraordinary they may have been for a moment, are gone forever, "melted into air, into thin air."

MORAL REGENERATION THROUGH ILLUSION

To look at the Elizabethan theatre through Shakespeare's internal plays is to, as Polonius advises, "by indirections find directions out." Seldom to be taken straight, these internal plays nonetheless reveal the aspects of presentation that regularly attracted Shakespeare's attention. His own professional actors were probably not as crude as Bottom's amateur players, nor were his plays by any means so old-fashioned as *The Murder of Gonzago*. Also, he probably never found actors as pliable and accommodating as Ariel and his company of spirits. But, as he portrays his players, his stage, and his audience ironically, he always returns to the same performance issues. Do the players perform badly? How realistic is the stage setting? Does the audience hear and see the play in the right imaginative spirit, and does it move them toward some kind of moral reformation? Is the play put together in an effective manner?

Sometimes the poet apologizes for the necessity of illusion on his bare stage, as does the Chorus in *Henry V*. Sometimes he laughs at excessive realism, as in *Pyramus and Thisbe*. At other times he laments the transience of theatrical illusion as Prospero does, and sometimes he mocks his audiences for failing to enter into the artificial reality of the creative imagination. But all his oblique comments on performance in his theatre show a relatively crude and limited performance on the actual stage contrasted with the powers of imagination, in the playwright's words and the audience's reception, to create understanding and moral regeneration through illusion.

Chapter 3

TRAGEDY IN SHAKESPEARE'S TIME

*T*he long hiatus in the history of tragedy between the Greeks and the Elizabethans has been variously explained. In the Golden Age of Roman literature, roughly from the birth of Virgil in 70 BCE to the death of Ovid in 17 CE, the Roman poets followed the example of Greek literature. Although they produced great lyric and epic verse, their tragic drama lacked the probing freshness and directness fundamental to tragedy. With the collapse of the Roman world and the invasions of the barbarians came the beginnings of the long, slow development of the Christian church. Churchmen and philosophers gradually forged a system, based on Christian revelation, of human nature and destiny. The mass, with its daily reenactment of the sacrifice of Jesus Christ, its music, and its dramatic structure, may have provided something comparable to tragic drama in the lives of the people.

With the coming of the Renaissance, the visual arts more and more came to represent the afflictive aspects of life, and the word *tragedy* again came into currency. Geoffrey Chaucer used the word in *Troilus and Criseyde*, and in *The Canterbury Tales* it is applied to a series of stories in the medieval style of *de casibus virorum illustrium*, meaning "the downfalls (more or less inevitable) of princes." Chaucer used the word to signify little more than the turn of the wheel of fortune, against whose force no meaningful human effort is possible. It remained for the Elizabethans

Portrait of Geoffrey Chaucer astride a horse. Chaucer helped revive the term "tragedy" as it pertains to certain dramatic theatrical works. Hulton Archive/Getty Images

to develop a theatre and a dramatic literature that reinstated the term on a level comparable to that of the Greeks.

ELIZABETHAN TRAGEDY

The long beginning of the Elizabethan popular theatre, like that of the Greek theatre, lay in religious ceremonials, probably in the drama in the liturgy of the two greatest events in the Christian year, Christmas and Easter. In the early church, exchanges between two groups of choristers, or between the choir and a solo voice, led to the idea of dialogue, just as it had in the development of Greek tragedy. The parts became increasingly elaborate, and costumes were introduced to individualize the characters. Dramatic gestures and actions were a natural development. More and more of the biblical stories were dramatized, much as the material of Homer was used by the Greek tragedians, although piously in this instance, with none of the tragic skepticism of the Greeks.

In the course of generations, the popularity of the performances grew to such an extent that, to accommodate the crowds, they were moved, from inside the church to the porch, or square, in front of the church. The next step was the secularization of the management of the productions, as the towns and cities took them over. Daylong festivals were instituted, involving, as in the Greek theatre, the whole community. Cycles of plays were performed at York, Chester, and other English religious centres, depicting in sequences of short dramatic episodes the whole human story, from the Fall of Lucifer and the Creation to the Day of Doom. Each play was assigned to an appropriate trade guild (the story of Noah

Actors from a modern-day theatre troupe perform from a wagon bed during the annual York Festival in England. In Shakespeare's time, cyclical plays were staged during similar festivals by theatrical guilds. Visit Britain/Britain on View/Getty Images

and the Ark, for example, went to the shipwrights), which took over complete responsibility for the production. Hundreds of actors and long preparation went into the festivals. These "miracle" and "mystery" plays, however crude they may now seem, dealt with the loftiest of subjects in simple but often powerful eloquence. Although the audience must have been a motley throng, it may well have been as involved and concerned as those of the Greek theatre.

Once the drama became a part of the secular life of the communities, popular tastes affected its religious orientation. Comic scenes, like those involving Noah's nagging wife, a purely secular creation who does

not appear in the Bible, became broader. The "tragic" scenes—anything involving the Devil or Doomsday—became more and more melodramatic. With the Renaissance came the rediscovery of the Greek and Roman cultures and the consequent development of a world view that led away from moral and spiritual absolutes and toward an increasingly skeptical individualism. The high poetic spirits of the mid-16th century began to turn the old medieval forms of the miracles and mysteries to new uses and to look to the ancient plays, particularly the lurid tragedies of Seneca, for their models. A bloody play, *Gorboduc*, by Thomas Sackville and Thomas Norton, first acted in 1561, is now known as the first formal tragedy in English, though it is far from fulfilling the high offices of the form in tone, characterization, and theme. Thomas Kyd's *Spanish Tragedy* (*c.* 1587) continued the Senecan tradition of the "tragedy of blood" with somewhat more sophistication than *Gorboduc* but even more

Reproduction of the frontpiece from a 1615 edition of Thomas Kyd's *The Spanish Tragedy. Characters brandishing swords and torches hint at the bloody nature of this tragic work.* Universal Images Group/ Getty Images

bloodletting. Elizabethan tragedy never freed itself completely from certain melodramatic aspects of the influence of Seneca.

CHRISTOPHER MARLOWE AND THE FIRST CHRISTIAN TRAGEDY

The first tragedian worthy of the tradition of the Greeks was Christopher Marlowe. Of Marlowe's trage-dies, *Tamburlaine* (1587), *Doctor Faustus* (c. 1588), *The Jew*

CHRISTOPHER MARLOWE

Shakespeare's most important predecessor in English drama was Elizabethan poet and playwright Christopher Marlowe, who is noted especially for his establishment of dramatic blank verse.

Baptized Feb. 26, 1564 in Canterbury, England, Marlowe was the son of a Canterbury shoemaker. Nothing is known of his early schooling, but in 1579 he entered the King's School, Canterbury, as a scholar. A year later he went to Corpus Christi College, Cambridge. Obtaining a bachelor of arts degree in 1584, he continued in residence at Cambridge, which may imply that he was intending to take Anglican

Portrait of Shakespeare's contemporary Christopher Marlowe. Keystone/Hulton Archive/Getty Images

orders. In 1587, however, the university hesitated about granting him the master's degree. Its doubts (arising from his frequent absences from the university) were apparently set to rest when the Privy Council sent a letter declaring that he had been employed "on matters touching the benefit of his country"—apparently in Elizabeth I's secret service.

After 1587 Marlowe was in London, writing for the theatres, occasionally getting into trouble with the authorities because of his violent and disreputable behaviour, and probably also engaging himself from time to time in government service. Marlowe won a dangerous reputation for "atheism," but this could, in Elizabeth I's time, indicate merely unorthodox religious opinions. In Robert Greene's deathbed tract, *Greenes groats-worth of witte,* Marlowe is referred to as a "famous gracer of Tragedians" and is reproved for having said, like Greene himself, "There is no god" and for having studied "pestilent Machiuilian pollicie" (Machiavellian policy, i.e., marked by cunning, duplicity, or bad faith). On May 30, 1593, Marlowe was killed, in dubious company, at a lodging house in Deptford, where it was alleged a fight broke out over the bill.

of Malta (1589), and *Edward II* (c. 1593), the first two are the most famous and most significant.

In *Tamburlaine*, the material was highly melodramatic. The popular image of the Central Asian conqueror Timur (or Timur Lenk ["Timur the Lame"]; known in English as Tamerlane or Tamberlaine) was that of the most ruthless and bloody of conquerors. In a verse prologue, when Marlowe invites the audience to "View but his [Tamburlaine's] picture in this tragic glass," he had in mind little more, perhaps, than the trappings and tone of tragedy: "the stately tent of war," which is to be his scene, and "the high astounding terms," which will be his rhetoric. But he brought such imaginative vigour and sensitivity to bear that melodrama is transcended, in terms reminiscent of high tragedy. Tamburlaine, a Scythian shepherd of the 14th century, becomes the spokesman, curiously enough, for the new world of the Renaissance—iconoclastic, independent, stridently ambitious. Just as the Greek tragedians challenged tradition, Tamburlaine shouts defiance at all the norms, religious and moral, that Marlowe's generation inherited. But Tamburlaine, although he is an iconoclast, is also a poet. No one before him on the English stage had talked with such magnificent lyric power as he does, whether it be on the glories of conquest or on the beauties of Zenocrate, his beloved. When, still unconquered by any enemy, he sickens and dies, he leaves the feeling that something great, however ruthless, has gone. Here once again is the ambiguity that was so much a part of the Greek tragic imagination—the combination of awe, pity, and fear that Aristotle defined.

Faustus, detail from the title page of the 1616 edition of The Tragical History of Dr. Faustus *by Christopher Marlowe.* Courtesy of the trustees of the British Library; photograph, R.B. Fleming

In *Doctor Faustus* the sense of conflict between the tradition and the new Renaissance individualism is much greater. The claims of revealed Christianity are presented in the orthodox spirit of the morality and mystery plays, but Faustus's yearnings for power over space and time are also presented with a sympathy that cannot be denied. Here is modern man, tragic modern man, torn between the faith of tradition and faith in himself. Faustus takes the risk in the end and is bundled off to hell in true mystery-play fashion. But the final scene does not convey that justice has been done, even though Faustus admits that his fate is just. Rather, the scene suggests that the transcendent human individual has been caught in the consequences of a dilemma that he might have avoided but that no imaginative man *could* have avoided.

The sense of the interplay of fate and freedom is not unlike that of *Oedipus*. The sense of tragic ambiguity is more poignant in Faustus than in Oedipus or Tamburlaine because Faustus is far more introspective than either of the other heroes. The conflict is inner; the battle is for Faustus's soul, a kind of conflict that neither the Greeks nor Tamburlaine had to contend with. For this reason, and not because it advocates Christian doctrine, the play has been called the first Christian tragedy.

SHAKESPEAREAN TRAGEDY

Shakespeare was a long time coming to his tragic phase, the seven or so years that produced his five greatest tragedies—*Hamlet*, *Othello*, *King Lear*, *Macbeth*, and *Antony and Cleopatra*. These were not the only plays he wrote during the first years of the 17th century. *Troilus and Cressida* may have come about the same time as or shortly after *Hamlet*, *All's Well That Ends Well* shortly before or after *Othello*, and *Measure for Measure* shortly before *King Lear*. But the concentration of tragedies is sufficient to distinguish this period from that of the comedies and history plays before and that of the so-called romances afterward.

Although the tragic period cannot entirely be accounted for in terms of biography, social history, or current stage fashions, all of which have been adduced as causes, certain questions should be answered, at least tentatively: What is Shakespeare's major tragic theme and method? How do they relate to Classical, medieval, and Renaissance traditions? In attempting to answer these questions, this proviso must be kept in mind: The degree to which he was consciously working in these traditions, consciously shaping his plays on early models, adapting Greek and Roman themes to his own purpose, or following the precepts of Aristotle must always remain conjectural. On the one hand, there is the comment by Ben Jonson that Shakespeare had "small Latin and less Greek," and John Milton in *L'Allegro* speaks of him as "fancy's child" warbling "his native wood-notes wild," as if he were unique, a sport of nature. On the other hand, Shakespeare knew Jonson (who knew a great deal of Latin and Greek) and is said to have acted in Jonson's *Sejanus* in 1603, a very Classical play, published in 1605 with a learned essay on Aristotle as preface.

It can be assumed that Shakespeare knew the tradition. Certainly the Elizabethan theatre could not have existed without the Greek and Roman prototype. For all of its mixed nature—with comic and melodramatic elements jostling the tragic—the Elizabethan theatre retained some of the high concern, the sense of involvement, and even the ceremonial atmosphere of the Greek theatre. When tragedies were performed, the stage was draped in black. Modern studies have shown that the Elizabethan theatre retained many ties with both the Middle Ages and the tradition of the Greeks.

FROM COMEDY TO TRAGEDY

Shakespeare's earliest and most lighthearted plays reveal a sense of the individual, his innerness, his reality, his difference from every other individual, and, at times, his plight. Certain stock characters, to be sure, appear in the early comedies. Even Falstaff, that triumphant individual, has a prototype in the braggadocio of Roman comedy, and even Falstaff has his tragic side. As Shakespeare's art developed, his concern for the plight or predicament or

HUNTINGTON CITY TOWNSHIP
PUBLIC LIBRARY
255 WEST PARK DRIVE
HUNTINGTON, IN 46750

Actors portraying (foreground, left to right) *Falstaff and Prince Hal in a 1970 production of* Henry V, Part 1. *A comic figure, Falstaff nonetheless exhibits a dark side, commenting on political intrigue and war.* Michael Webb/Hulton Archive/Getty Images

dilemma seems to have grown. His earliest history plays, for instance (*Henry VI*, Parts 1, 2, and 3), are little more than chronicles of the great pageant figures—kingship in all its colour and potency. *Richard III* (1592–94), which follows them, focuses with an intensity traditionally reserved for the tragic hero on one man and on the sinister forces, within and without, that bring him to destruction. From kingship, that is, Shakespeare turned to the king, the symbolic individual, the focal man, to whom whole societies look for their values and meanings. Thus Richard III is almost wholly sinister, though there exists a fascination about him, an all but tragic ambiguity.

Although Shakespeare's developing sense of the tragic cannot be summed up adequately in any formula, one might hazard the following: he progressed from the *individual* of the early comedies; to the *burdened* individual, such as, in *Henry IV*, Prince Hal, the future Henry V, who manipulates, rather than suffers, the tragic ambiguities of the world; and, finally, in the great tragedies, to (in one critic's phrase) the *overburdened* individual, Lear being generally regarded as the greatest example. In these last plays, man is at the limits of his sovereignty as a human being, where everything that he has lived by, stood for, or loved is put to the test. Like Prometheus on the crag, or Oedipus as he learns who he is, or Medea deserted by Jason, the Shakespearean tragic heroes are at the extremities of their natures. Hamlet and Macbeth are thrust to the very edge of sanity; Lear and, momentarily, Othello are thrust beyond it. In every case, as in the Greek plays, the destructive forces seem to combine inner inadequacies or evils, such as Lear's temper or Macbeth's ambition, with external pressures, such as Lear's "tiger daughters," the witches in *Macbeth*, or Lady Macbeth's importunity. Once the destructive course is set going, these forces operate with the relentlessness the Greeks called *moira*, or Fate.

THE FATES

In Greek and Roman mythology, the Fates were three goddesses who determined human destinies, and in particular the span of a person's life and his allotment of misery and suffering. Homer speaks of Fate (*moira*) in the singular as an impersonal power and sometimes makes its functions interchangeable with those of the Olympian gods. From the time of the poet Hesiod (8th century BCE) on, however, the Fates were personified as three very old women who spin the threads of human destiny. Their names were Clotho (Spinner), Lachesis (Allotter), and Atropos (Inflexible). Clotho spun the "thread" of human fate, Lachesis dispensed it, and Atropos cut the thread (thus determining the individual's moment of death).

The Romans identified the Parcae, originally personifications of childbirth, with the three Greek Fates. The Roman goddesses were named Nona, Decuma, and Morta.

Italian artist Correggio's depiction of the Parcae, *or the Roman goddesses of fate.* © De Agostini/SuperStock

SHAKESPEARE'S TRAGIC ART

At the height of his powers, Shakespeare revealed a tragic vision that comprehended the totality of possibilities for good and evil as nearly as the human imagination ever has. His heroes are the vehicles of psychological, societal, and cosmic forces that tend to ennoble and glorify humanity or infect it and destroy it. The logic of tragedy that possessed him demanded an insistence upon the latter. Initially, his heroes make free choices and are free time after time to turn back, but they move toward their doom as relentlessly as did Oedipus.

The total tragic statement, however, is not limited to the fate of the hero. He is but the centre of an action that takes place in a context involving many other characters, each contributing a point of view, a set of values or anti-values to the complex dialectic of the play. In Macbeth's demon-ridden Scotland, where weird things happen to men and horses turn cannibal, there is the virtuous Malcolm, and society survives. Hamlet had the trustworthy friend Horatio, and, for all the bloodletting, what was "rotten" was purged. In the tragedies, most notably *Lear*, the Aeschylean notion of "knowledge through suffering" is powerfully dramatized. It is most obvious in the hero, but it is also shared by the society of which he is the focal figure. The flaw in the hero may be a moral failing or, sometimes, an excess of virtue. The flaw in society may be the rottenness of the Danish court in *Hamlet* or the corruption of the Roman world in *Antony and Cleopatra*. The flaw or fault or dislocation may be in the very universe itself, as dramatized by Lear's raving at the heavens or the ghosts that walk the plays or the witches that prophesy. All these faults, Shakespeare seems to be saying, are inevitabilities of the human condition. But they do not spell rejection, nihilism, or despair. The hero may die, but, in the words of the novelist E.M. Forster to describe the redeeming power of tragedy, "he has given us life."

Such is the precarious balance a tragedian must maintain: the cold, clear vision that sees the evil but is not maddened by it, a sense of the good that is equally clear but refuses the blandishments of optimism or sentimentalism. Few have ever sustained the balance for long. Aeschylus tended to slide off to the right, Euripides to the left, and even Sophocles had his hero transfigured at Colonus. Marlowe's early death should perhaps spare him the criticism his first plays warrant. Shakespeare's last two tragedies, *Macbeth* and *Antony and Cleopatra*, are close to the edge of a valueless void. The atmosphere of *Macbeth* is murky with evil. The action moves with almost melodramatic speed from horror to horror. The forces for good rally at last, but Macbeth himself steadily deteriorates into the most nihilistic of all Shakespeare's tragic heroes, saved in nothing except the sense of a great nature, like Medea, gone wrong. *Antony and Cleopatra*, in its ambiguities and irony, has been considered close to the Euripidean line of bitterness and detachment.

Shakespeare himself soon modulated into another mood in his last plays, *Cymbeline*, *The Winter's Tale*, and *The Tempest*. Each is based on a situation that could have been developed into major tragedy had Shakespeare followed out its logic as he had done with earlier plays. For whatever reason, however, he chose not to. The great tragic questions are not pressed. As a result, these late plays are generally classified, for better or worse, as romances and are shoehorned into the category of comedies. Yet *The Tempest*, especially, for all Prospero's charm and magnanimity, gives a sense of brooding melancholy over the ineradicable evil in humankind, a patient but sad acquiescence. All of these plays end in varying degrees of harmony and reconciliation. Shakespeare willed it so.

DECLINE IN 17TH-CENTURY ENGLAND

From Shakespeare's tragedies to the closing of the theatres in England by the Puritans in 1642, the quality of tragedy was steadily worse, if the best of the Greek and Shakespearean tragedies are taken as a standard. Among the leading dramatists of the period—John Webster, Thomas Middleton, Francis Beaumont, John Fletcher, Cyril Tourneur, and John Ford—there were some excellent craftsmen and brilliant poets. Though each of them has a rightful place in the history of English drama, tragedy suffered a transmutation in their hands.

The Jacobean dramatists—those who flourished in England during the reign of James I—failed to transcend the negative tendencies they inherited from Elizabethan tragedy: a sense of defeat, a mood of spiritual despair implicit in Marlowe's tragic thought. This is evident in the nihilistic broodings of some of Shakespeare's characters in their worst moods—Hamlet, Gloucester in *Lear*, Macbeth--and in the metaphoric implication of the theme of insanity, of a man pressed beyond the limit of endurance, that runs through many of these tragedies. Most importantly, perhaps, it is seen in the moral confusion ("fair is foul and foul is fair") that threatens to unbalance even the staunchest of Shakespeare's tragic heroes.

This sinister tendency came to a climax about 1605 and was in part a consequence of the anxiety surrounding the death of Queen Elizabeth I and the accession of James I. Despite their negative tendencies, the Elizabethans, in general, had affirmed life and celebrated it. Shakespeare's moral balance, throughout even his darkest plays, remained firm. The Jacobeans, on the other hand, were possessed by death. They became superb analysts of moral confusion and of the darkened vision of humanity at cross purposes, preying upon itself; of lust, hate, and intrigue engulfing what is left of beauty, love, and integrity. There is little that is redemptive or that suggests, as had Aeschylus, that evil might be resolved by the enlightenment gained from suffering. As in the tragedies of Euripides, the protagonist's margin of freedom grows ever smaller. "You are the deed's creature," cries a murderer to his unwitting lady accomplice in Middleton's *Changeling* (1622), and a prisoner of her deed she remains. Many of the plays maintained a pose of ironic, detached reportage, without the sense of sympathetic involvement that the greatest tragedians have conveyed from the beginning.

Some of the qualities of the highest tragedians have been claimed for John Webster. One critic points to his search for a moral order as a link to Shakespeare and sees in his moral vision a basis for renewal. Webster's *Duchess of Malfi* (c. 1612–13) has been interpreted as a final triumph

British actor Michael Redgrave as a bound Samson, with Faith Brooks as Delilah, in a scene from Samson Agonistes, *a play by the poet John Milton.* Hulton Archive/Getty Images

of life over death. Overwhelmed by final unleashed terror, the Duchess affirms the essential dignity of man. Despite such vestiges of greatness, however, the trend of tragedy was downward. High moral sensitivity and steady conviction are required to resist the temptation to resolve the intolerable tensions of tragedy into either the comfort of optimism or the relaxed apathy of despair. Periods of the creation of high tragedy are therefore few and short-lived. The demands on artist and audience alike are very great. Forms wear out, and public taste seems destined to go through inevitable cycles of health and disease. What is to one generation powerful and persuasive rhetoric becomes bombast and bathos to the next. The inevitable materials of tragedy—violence, madness, hate, and lust—soon lose their symbolic role and become perverted to the uses of melodrama and sensationalism, mixed, for relief, with the broadest comedy or farce.

These corruptions had gone too far when John Milton, 29 years after the closing of the theatres, attempted to bring back the true spirit and tone of tragedy, which he called "the gravest, moralest, and most profitable of all other Poems." His *Samson Agonistes* (1671), however, is magnificent "closet tragedy"—drama more suitable for reading than for popular performance. Modeled on the *Prometheus*, it recalls Aeschylus's tragedy both in its form, in which the immobilized hero receives a sequence of visitors, and in its theme, in which there is a resurgence of the hero's spirit under stress. With Restoration comedy in full swing, however, and with the "heroic play" (an overly moralized version of tragedy) about to reach its crowning achievement in John Dryden's *All for Love* only seven years later (published 1678), *Samson Agonistes* was an anachronism.

Chapter 4

INSIDE THE PLAYS: SHAKESPEARE'S TRAGEDIES

*T*he confusions and contradictions of Shakespeare's age find their highest expression in his tragedies. In these extraordinary achievements, all values, hierarchies, and forms are tested and found wanting, and all society's latent conflicts are activated. Shakespeare sets husband against wife, father against child, the individual against society. He uncrowns kings, levels the nobleman with the beggar, and interrogates the gods.

Already in the early experimental tragedies *Titus Andronicus*, with its spectacular violence, and *Romeo and Juliet,* with its comedy and romantic tale of adolescent love, Shakespeare had broken away from the conventional Elizabethan understanding of tragedy as a twist of fortune to an infinitely more complex investigation of character and motive. In *Julius Caesar,* he begins to turn the political interests of the history plays into secular and corporate tragedy, as men fall victim to the unstoppable train of public events set in motion by their private misjudgments. In the major tragedies that follow, Shakespeare's practice cannot be confined to a single general statement that covers all cases, for each tragedy belongs to a separate category: revenge tragedy in *Hamlet*, domestic tragedy in *Othello*, social tragedy in *King Lear,* political tragedy in *Macbeth*, and heroic tragedy in *Antony and Cleopatra.*

This chapter discusses the tragedies in a general fashion, and summarizes each play individually.

REVENGE TRAGEDY

Revenge tragedy—drama in which the dominant motive is revenge for a real or imagined injury—was a favourite form of tragedy in the Elizabethan and Jacobean eras. It derived originally from the Roman tragedies of Seneca. The genre was established on the English stage by Thomas Kyd with *The Spanish Tragedy* (*c.* 1587). This work, which opens with the Ghost of Andrea and Revenge, deals with Hieronimo, a Spanish gentleman who is driven to melancholy by the murder of his son. Between spells of madness, he discovers who the murderers are and plans his ingenious revenge. He stages a play in which the murderers take part, and, while enacting his role, Hieronimo actually kills them, then kills himself.

The influence of this play, so apparent in *Hamlet*, is also evident in other plays of the period. In John Marston's *Antonio's Revenge* (1599–1601), the ghost of Antonio's slain father urges Antonio to avenge his murder, which Antonio does during a court masque. In George Chapman's *Revenge of Bussy d'Ambois* (performed *c.* 1610), Bussy's ghost begs his introspective brother Clermont to avenge his murder. Clermont hesitates and vacillates but at last complies, then kills himself.

Most revenge tragedies end with a scene of carnage that disposes of the avenger as well as his victims. Other examples are Shakespeare's *Titus Andronicus* (performed 1589–92), Henry Chettle's *Tragedy of Hoffman* (performed 1602), and Thomas Middleton's *Revenger's Tragedy* (1607).

THE EARLY TRAGEDIES

Shakespeare arrived in London probably sometime in the late 1580s. He was in his mid-20s. It is not known how he got started in the theatre or for what acting companies he wrote his early plays, which are not easy to date. Indicating a time of apprenticeship, these plays show a more direct debt to London dramatists of the 1580s and to Classical examples than do his later works. He learned a great deal about writing plays by imitating the successes of the London theatre, as any young poet and budding dramatist might do.

TITUS ANDRONICUS

An early, experimental tragedy, *Titus Andronicus* was written sometime between 1589 and 1592, and published in a quarto edition from an incomplete draft in 1594. The First Folio version was prepared from a copy of the quarto, with additions from a manuscript that had been used as a promptbook. The play's crude, melodramatic style and its numerous savage incidents led many critics to believe it was not written by Shakespeare. Modern criticism, however, tends to regard the play as authentic.

Although not ranked with Shakespeare's other great Roman plays, *Titus Andronicus* relates its story of revenge and political strife with a uniformity of tone and consistency of dramatic structure. Sources for the story include Euripides' *Hecuba*, Seneca's *Thyestes and Troades*, and parts of Ovid and Plutarch. More important, an 18th-century chapbook titled *The History of Titus Andronicus*, though clearly too late to have served as Shakespeare's source, may well have been derived from a closely similar prose version that Shakespeare could have known.

Titus Andronicus returns to Rome after having defeated the Goths, bringing with him Queen Tamora, whose eldest son he sacrifices to the gods. The late emperor's son Saturninus is supposed to marry Titus's daughter Lavinia. However, when his brother Bassianus

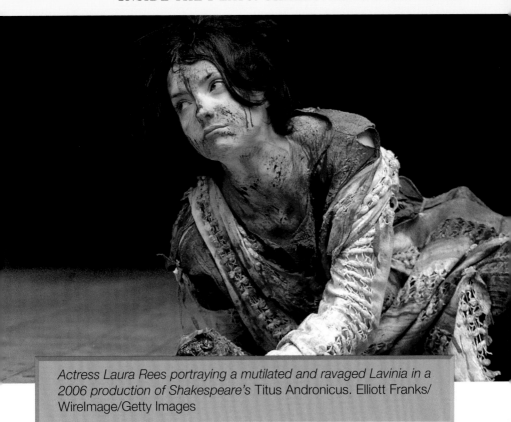

Actress Laura Rees portraying a mutilated and ravaged Lavinia in a 2006 production of Shakespeare's Titus Andronicus. Elliott Franks/ WireImage/Getty Images

runs away with her instead, Saturninus marries Tamora. Saturninus and Tamora then plot revenge against Titus. Lavinia is raped and mutilated by Tamora's sadistic sons Demetrius and Chiron, who cut off her hands and cut out her tongue so that she will be unable to testify against them. She nonetheless manages, by holding a stick in her mouth and guiding it with the stumps of her hands, to reveal the names of her ravishers. Tamora, meanwhile takes as her lover an African man named Aaron the Moor. They produce a mixed-race child of whom Aaron is intensely proud.

Titus now emerges as the revenger who must bring Tamora's brutal family to account. Titus's garish revenge begins as he puts on the guise of madness. He pretends to

THOMAS KYD

(baptized Nov. 6, 1558, London, England—d. *c.* December 1594, London)

The English dramatist Thomas Kyd, with his play *The Spanish Tragedy* (sometimes called *Hieronimo*, or *Jeronimo*, after its protagonist), initiated the revenge tragedy of his day. He anticipated the structure of many later plays, including the development of middle and final climaxes. In addition, he revealed an instinctive sense of tragic situation.

The son of a scrivener, Kyd was educated at the Merchant Taylors School in London. There is no evidence that he attended the university before turning to literature. He seems to have been in service for some years with a lord (possibly Ferdinando, Lord Strange, the patron of Lord Strange's Men). *The Spanish Tragedy* was entered in the Stationers' Register in October 1592, and the undated first quarto edition almost certainly appeared in that year. It is not known which company first played it, nor when; but Strange's company played *Hieronimo* 16 times in 1592, and the Admiral's Men revived it in 1597, as apparently did the Chamberlain's Men. It remained one of the most popular plays of the age and was often reprinted.

The only other play certainly by Kyd is *Cornelia* (1594), an attempt at Senecan tragedy, translated from the French of Robert Garnier's academic *Cornélie*. He may also have written an earlier version of *Hamlet*, known to scholars as "the Ur-Hamlet," and his hand has sometimes been detected in the anonymous *Arden of Feversham*, one of the first domestic tragedies, and in a number of other plays.

About 1591 Kyd was sharing lodgings with Christopher Marlowe, and on May 13, 1593, he was arrested and then tortured, being suspected of treasonable activity. His room had been searched and certain "atheistical" disputations denying the deity of Jesus Christ found there. He probably averred then and certainly confirmed later, in a letter, that these papers had belonged to Marlowe. That letter is the source for almost everything that is known about Kyd's life. He was dead by Dec. 30, 1594, when his mother made a formal repudiation of her son's debt-ridden estate.

accept Demetrius and Chiron as the personifications of Rape and Murder, invites them into his house, and murders them, with Lavinia holding a basin to catch their blood. Titus then prepares a feast in which, acting as cook, he serves up to Tamora her own sons baked in a dish. Titus kills Lavinia to end her shame, stabs Tamora, and is cut down by Saturninus, at which Titus's son Lucius responds by delivering Saturninus a fatal blow. Aaron the Moor is to be executed as well for his villainies. The blood-filled stage is presided over finally by Lucius and Titus's brother, Marcus, as the sole survivors of Titus's much-wronged family.

As has been suggested, Shakespeare's first full-length tragedy owes much of its theme, structure, and language to Thomas Kyd's *The Spanish Tragedy*, which was a huge success in the late 1580s. Kyd had hit on the formula of adopting the dramaturgy of Seneca the Younger, the great Stoic philosopher and statesman, to the needs of a burgeoning new London theatre. This adaptation resulted in a genre known as revenge tragedy. Shakespeare also borrowed a leaf from his great contemporary Christopher Marlowe. The Vice-like protagonist of Marlowe's *The Jew of Malta*, Barabas, may have inspired Shakespeare in his depiction of the villainous Aaron the Moor in *Titus Andronicus*, though other Vice figures were available to him as well.

ROMEO AND JULIET

Shakespeare's tragedy *Romeo and Juliet* was written about 1594–96 and first published in an unauthorized quarto in 1597. An authorized quarto appeared in 1599, substantially longer and more reliable. A third quarto, based on the second, was used by the editors of the First Folio of 1623. The characters of Romeo and Juliet have been depicted in literature, music, dance, and theatre. The appeal of the young hero and heroine—whose families, the Montagues and the Capulets, respectively, are implacable enemies—is such that they have become, in the popular imagination, the representative type of star-crossed lovers.

Shakespeare's principal source for the plot was *The Tragicall Historye of Romeus and Juliet* (1562), a long narrative poem by the English poet Arthur Brooke, who had based his poem on a French translation of a tale by the Italian Matteo Bandello.

Shakespeare sets the scene in Verona, Italy. Juliet and Romeo meet and fall instantly in love at a masked ball of the Capulets, and they profess their love when Romeo, unwilling to leave, climbs the wall into the orchard garden of her family's house and finds her alone at her window. Because their well-to-do families are enemies, the two are married secretly by Friar Laurence. When Tybalt, a Capulet, seeks out Romeo in revenge for the insult of Romeo's having dared to shower his attentions on Juliet, an ensuing scuffle ends in the death of Romeo's dearest friend, Mercutio. Impelled by a code of honour among men, Romeo kills Tybalt and is banished to Mantua by the Prince of Verona, who has been insistent that the family feuding cease.

Unaware that Juliet is already secretly married, Juliet's father arranges a marriage with the eminently eligible Count Paris. The young bride seeks out Friar Laurence

WEST SIDE STORY

The movie *West Side Story* (1961) was conceived, directed, and choreographed by American choreographer Jerome Robbins, who envisioned it as a contemporary musical update of Shakespeare's *Romeo and Juliet*. His original idea was for the young star-crossed lovers to be from differing religious backgrounds, with an Italian Catholic Romeo and a Jewish Juliet.

Fight scene from West Side Story. Courtesy of United Artists Corporation

This backdrop was abandoned, however, for one of warring teenage Puerto Rican and American gangs. The screenplay was written by Ernest Lehman and based on the stage play of the same name by Arthur Laurents (1957).

The play opened on Broadway in September 1957 to great success. When the film was cast, however, most of the Broadway actors were rejected for looking too old to play teenagers. Although Anthony Perkins, Warren Beatty, Suzanne Pleshette, and Jill St. John, among others, tested for the lead roles, Richard Beymer was ultimately cast as Tony (with singing dubbed by Jimmy Bryant) and Natalie Wood as Maria (with singing dubbed by Marni Nixon). The movie is filled with explosive dance sequences, and the memorable songs by composers Leonard Bernstein and Stephen Sondheim include "Tonight," "Maria," and "Somewhere." The film won 10 of the 11 Academy Awards for which it was nominated, and Robbins received an honorary award for his choreography.

for assistance in her desperate situation. He gives her a potion that will make her appear to be dead and proposes that she take it and that Romeo rescue her. She complies. Romeo, however, unaware of the friar's scheme because a letter has failed to reach him, returns to Verona on hearing of Juliet's apparent death. He reluctantly kills a grieving Paris, who attempts to prevent Romeo from entering Juliet's tomb, and finds Juliet in the burial vault. There he gives her a last kiss and kills himself with poison. Juliet awakens, sees the dead Romeo, and kills herself. Upon learning what has happened, the chastened families end their feud.

JULIUS CAESAR

Shakespeare's tragedy *Julius Caesar* is also classifiable as a history play. It was produced in 1599–1600 and published in the First Folio of 1623 from a transcript of a promptbook.

Based on Sir Thomas North's 1579 translation (via a French version) of Plutarch's *Bioi parallēloi* (*Parallel Lives*), the drama takes place in 44 BCE, after Caesar has

JULIUS CAESAR THE MAN

(b. July 12/13, 100? BCE, Rome [Italy]—d. March 15, 44 BCE, Rome)

The historical Julius Caesar was a celebrated Roman general and statesman, the conqueror of Gaul (58–50 BCE), victor in the Civil War of 49–45 BCE, and dictator (46–44 BCE), who was launching a series of political and social reforms when he was assassinated by a group of nobles in the Senate House on the Ides of March. His family name, Caesar, has come to signify a ruler who is in some sense uniquely supreme or paramount—the meaning of Kaiser in German, tsar in the Slavonic languages, and qayṣar in Arabic. His gens (clan) name, Julius (Iulius), is also familiar in the Christian world. In Caesar's lifetime the Roman month Quintilis, in which he was born, was renamed "July" in his honour. This name has survived, as has Caesar's reform of the calendar. The old Roman calendar was inaccurate and manipulated for political purposes. Caesar's calendar, the Julian calendar, is still partially in force in the Eastern Orthodox Christian countries. And the Gregorian calendar, now in use in the West, is the Julian, slightly corrected by Pope Gregory XIII.

This cool-headed man of genius with an erratic vein of sexual exuberance undoubtedly changed the course of history. By liquidating the scandalous and bankrupt rule of the Roman nobility, he gave the Roman state—and with it the Greco-Roman civilization—a reprieve that lasted for more than 600 years in the East and for more than 400 years in the relatively backward West. If he had not done this when he did it, Rome and the Greco-Roman world might have succumbed, before the beginning of the Common Era, to barbarian invaders in the West and to the Parthian Empire in the East. The prolongation of the life of the Greco-Roman civilization had important historical effects. Under the Roman Empire the Middle East was impregnated with Hellenism for six or seven more centuries. But for this the Hellenic element might not have been present in sufficient strength to make its decisive impact on Christianity and Islam. Gaul, too, would have sunk deeper into barbarism when the Franks overran it, if it had not been associated with the civilized Mediterranean world for more than 500 years as a result of Caesar's conquest.

returned to Rome. Fearing Caesar's ambition, Cassius forms a conspiracy among Roman republicans. He persuades the reluctant Brutus, Caesar's trusted friend, to join them. Brutus, troubled and sleepless, finds comfort in the companionship of his noble wife, Portia. Caesar's wife, Calpurnia, alarmed by prophetic dreams, warns her husband not to go to the Capitol the next day. Then, as planned, Caesar is slain in the Senate on March 15, "the ides of March." His friend Mark Antony, who has expediently shaken the bloodied hands of the conspirators, gives a stirring funeral oration that inspires the crowd to turn against them. Octavius, Caesar's nephew, forms a triumvirate with Antony and Lepidus. Brutus and Cassius are eventually defeated at the Battle of Philippi, where they kill themselves to avoid further dishonour.

THE GREAT TRAGEDIES

One remarkable aspect of Shakespeare's great tragedies (*Hamlet, Othello, King Lear, Macbeth,* and *Antony and Cleopatra* most of all) is that they proceed through such a staggering range of human emotions, and especially the emotions that are appropriate to the mature years of the human cycle. Hamlet is 30, one learns—an age when a person is apt to perceive that the world around him is "an unweeded garden / That grows to seed. Things rank and gross in nature / Possess it merely" (Act I, scene 2, lines 135–137). Shakespeare was about 36 when he wrote this play. Othello centres on sexual jealousy in marriage. *King Lear* is about aging, generational conflict, and feelings of ingratitude. *Macbeth* explores ambition mad enough to kill a father figure who stands in the way. *Antony and Cleopatra*, written when Shakespeare was 42 or thereabouts, studies the exhilarating but ultimately dismaying phenomenon of midlife crisis. Shakespeare moves his readers vicariously through these life experiences while he himself struggles to capture, in tragic form, their terrors and challenges. These plays are deeply concerned with domestic and family relationships.

In each category Shakespeare's play is exemplary and defines its type. The range and brilliance of this achievement are staggering. The worlds of Shakespeare's heroes are collapsing around them, and their desperate attempts to cope with the collapse uncover the inadequacy of the systems by which they rationalize their sufferings and justify their existence. The ultimate insight is Lear's irremediable grief over his dead daughter: "Why should a dog, a horse, a rat have life, / And thou no breath at all?" Before the overwhelming suffering of these great and noble spirits, all consolations are void, and all versions of order stand revealed as adventitious. The humanism of the Renaissance is punctured in the very moment of its greatest single product.

HAMLET

Shakespeare wrote *Hamlet, Prince of Denmark* about 1599– 1601. It was published in a quarto edition in 1603 from an unauthorized text, with reference to an earlier play. The

First Folio version was taken from a second quarto of 1604 that was based on Shakespeare's own papers with some annotations by the bookkeeper of the Chamberlain's Men.

Shakespeare's telling of the story of Prince Hamlet was derived from several sources, notably from Books III and IV of Saxo Grammaticus's 12th-century *Gesta Danorum* and from volume 5 (1570) of *Histoires tragiques*, a free translation of *Saxo* by François de Belleforest. The play was evidently preceded by another play of Hamlet (now lost), usually referred to as "the Ur-Hamlet," of which Thomas Kyd is a conjectured author.

As Shakespeare's play opens, Hamlet is mourning his father, who has been killed, and lamenting the behaviour of his mother, Gertrude, who married his uncle Claudius within a month of his father's death. The ghost of his father appears to Hamlet, informs him that he was poisoned by

An illustration from a 19th-century edition of Hamlet, depicting Hamlet's encounter with his father's ghost during the night watch. Hulton Archive/Getty Images

Claudius, and commands Hamlet to avenge his death. Though instantly galvanized by the ghost's command, Hamlet decides on further reflection to seek evidence in corroboration of the ghostly visitation, since, he knows, the Devil can assume a pleasing shape and can easily mislead a person whose mind is perturbed by intense grief. Hamlet adopts a guise of melancholic and mad behaviour as a way of deceiving Claudius and others at court—a guise made all the easier by the fact that Hamlet is genuinely melancholic.

Hamlet's dearest friend, Horatio, agrees with him that Claudius has unambiguously confirmed his guilt. Driven by a guilty conscience, Claudius attempts to ascertain the cause of Hamlet's odd behaviour by hiring Hamlet's one-time friends Rosencrantz and Guildenstern to spy on him. Hamlet quickly sees through the scheme and begins to act the part of a madman in front of them. To the pompous old courtier Polonius, it appears that Hamlet is lovesick over Polonius's daughter Ophelia. Despite Ophelia's loyalty to him, Hamlet thinks that she, like everyone else, is turning against him. He feigns madness with her also and treats her cruelly as if she were representative, like his own mother, of her "treacherous" sex.

Hamlet contrives a plan to test the ghost's accusation. With a group of visiting actors, Hamlet arranges the performance of a story representing circumstances similar to those described by the ghost, under which Claudius poisoned Hamlet's father. When the play is presented as planned, the performance clearly unnerves Claudius.

Moving swiftly in the wake of the actors' performance, Hamlet confronts his mother in her chambers with her culpable loyalty to Claudius. When he hears a man's voice behind the curtains, Hamlet stabs the person he understandably assumes to be Claudius. The victim, however, is Polonius, who has been eavesdropping in an attempt to find out more about Hamlet's erratic behaviour. This act of violence persuades Claudius that his own life is in danger. He sends Hamlet to England escorted by Rosencrantz and Guildenstern, with secret orders that Hamlet be executed by the king of England. When Hamlet discovers the orders, he alters them to make his two friends the victims instead.

Upon his return to Denmark, Hamlet hears that Ophelia is dead of a suspected suicide (though more probably as a consequence of her having gone mad over her father's sudden death) and that her brother Laertes seeks to avenge Polonius's murder. Claudius is only too eager to arrange the duel. Carnage ensues. Hamlet dies of a wound inflicted by a sword that Claudius and Laertes have conspired to tip with poison. In the scuffle, Hamlet realizes what has happened and forces Laertes to exchange swords with him, so that Laertes too dies—as he admits, justly killed by his own treachery. Gertrude, also present at the duel, drinks from the cup of poison that Claudius has had placed near Hamlet to ensure his death. Before Hamlet himself dies, he manages to stab Claudius and to entrust the clearing of his honour to his friend Horatio.

In form, *Hamlet* is a revenge tragedy. It features characteristics also found in the earlier *Titus Andronicus*: a protagonist charged with the responsibility of avenging a heinous crime against his family, a cunning antagonist, the appearance of the ghost of the murdered person, the feigning of madness to throw off the villain's suspicions, the play within the play as a means of testing the villain, and still more. Yet to search out these comparisons is to highlight what is so extraordinary about *Hamlet*, for it refuses to be merely a revenge tragedy.

Shakespeare's protagonist is unique in the genre in his moral qualms, and most of all in his finding a way to carry out his dread command without becoming a cold-blooded murderer. Hamlet does act bloodily, especially when he kills Polonius, thinking that the old man hidden in Gertrude's chambers must be the King whom Hamlet is commissioned to kill. The act seems plausible and strongly motivated, and yet Hamlet sees at once that he has erred. He has killed the wrong man, even if Polonius has brought this on himself with his incessant spying. Hamlet sees that he has offended heaven and that he will have to pay for his act. When, at the play's end, Hamlet encounters his fate in a duel with Polonius's son, Laertes, Hamlet interprets his own tragic story as one that Providence has made meaningful. By placing himself in the hands of Providence and believing devoutly that "There's a divinity that shapes our ends, / Rough-hew them how we will" (Act V, scene 2, lines 10–11), Hamlet finds himself ready for a death that he has longed for. He also finds an opportunity for killing Claudius almost unpremeditatedly, spontaneously, as an act of reprisal for all that Claudius has done.

Hamlet thus finds tragic meaning in his own story. More broadly, too, he has searched for meaning in dilemmas of all sorts: his mother's overhasty marriage, Ophelia's dutiful succumbing to the will of her father and brother, his being spied on by his erstwhile friends Rosencrantz and Guildenstern, and much more. His utterances are often despondent, relentlessly honest, and philosophically profound, as he ponders the nature of friendship, memory, romantic attachment, filial love, sensuous enslavement, corrupting habits (drinking, sexual lust), and almost every phase of human experience.

OTHELLO

Shakespeare's tragedy *Othello, the Moor of Venice* was written in 1603–04 and published in 1622 in a quarto edition from a transcript of an authorial manuscript. The text published in the First Folio of 1623 seems to have been based on a version revised by Shakespeare himself that sticks close to the original almost line by line but introduces numerous substitutions of words and phrases, as though Shakespeare copied it over himself and rewrote as he copied. The play derives its plot from Giambattista Giraldi's *De gli Hecatommithi* (1565), which Shakespeare appears to have known in the Italian original. It was available to him in French but had not been translated into English.

The play is set in motion when Othello, a heroic black general in the service of Venice, appoints Cassio and not Iago as his chief lieutenant. Jealous of Othello's success and envious of Cassio, Iago plots Othello's downfall by falsely implicating Othello's wife, Desdemona, and Cassio in a love affair. With the unwitting aid of Emilia, his wife,

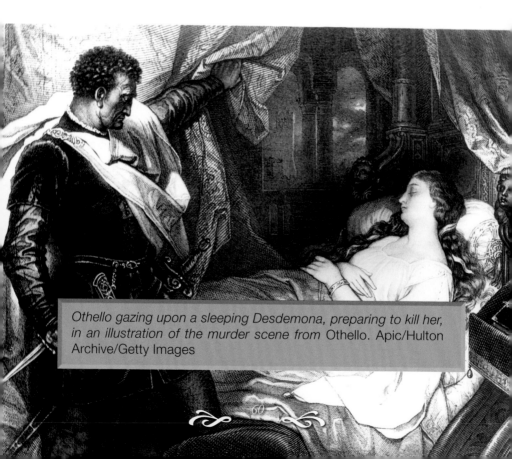

Othello gazing upon a sleeping Desdemona, preparing to kill her, in an illustration of the murder scene from Othello. Apic/Hulton Archive/Getty Images

and the willing help of Roderigo, a fellow malcontent, Iago carries out his plan. Making use of a handkerchief belonging to Desdemona and found by Emilia when Othello has unwittingly dropped it, Iago persuades Othello that Desdemona has given the handkerchief to Cassio as a love token. Iago also induces Othello to eavesdrop on a conversation between himself and Cassio that is in fact about Cassio's mistress, Bianca, but which Othello is led to believe concerns Cassio's infatuation with Desdemona. These slender "proofs" confirm what Othello has been all too inclined to believe—that, as an older black man, he is no longer attractive to his young white Venetian wife. Overcome with jealousy, Othello kills Desdemona. When he learns from Emilia, too late, that his wife is blameless, he asks to be remembered as one who "loved not wisely but too well" and kills himself.

This play is one of many plays that reveal Shakespeare's interest in the relationship between fathers and daughters as well as husbands and wives. Desdemona is the only daughter of Brabantio, an aging senator of Venice, who dies heartbroken because his daughter has eloped with a dark-skinned man who is her senior by many years and is of another culture. With Othello, Desdemona is briefly happy, despite her filial disobedience, until a terrible sexual jealousy is awakened in him, quite without cause other than his own fears and susceptibility to Iago's insinuations that it is only "natural" for Desdemona to seek erotic pleasure with a young man who shares her background. Driven by his own deeply irrational fear and hatred of women and seemingly mistrustful of his own masculinity, Iago can assuage his own inner torment only by persuading other men like Othello that their inevitable fate is to be cuckolded. As a tragedy, the play adroitly exemplifies the traditional Classical model of a good man brought to misfortune by hamartia, or tragic flaw.

It bears remembering, however, that Shakespeare owed no loyalty to this Classical model. *Hamlet,* for one, is a play that does not work well in Aristotelian terms. The search for an Aristotelian hamartia has led all too often to the trite argument that Hamlet suffers from melancholia and a tragic inability to act, whereas a more plausible reading of the play argues that finding the right course of action is highly problematic for him and for everyone. Hamlet sees examples on all sides of those whose forthright actions lead to fatal mistakes or absurd ironies (Laertes, Fortinbras), and indeed his own swift killing of the man he assumes to be Claudius hidden in his mother's chambers turns out to be a mistake for which he realizes he will be held accountable.

KING LEAR

Shakespeare's tragedy *King Lear* was written in 1605–06 and published in a quarto edition in 1608, evidently based on the author's unrevised working papers. The text of the First Folio of 1623 often differs markedly from the quarto text and seemingly represents a theatrical revision done by the author with some cuts designed for shortened performance.

The aging King Lear decides to divide his kingdom among his three daughters, allotting each a portion in proportion to the eloquence of her declaration of love. The hypocritical Goneril and Regan make grand pronouncements and are rewarded. Cordelia, the youngest daughter, who truly loves Lear, refuses to make an insincere speech to prove her love and is disinherited. The two older sisters mock Lear and soon renege on their promise to support him. Cast out, the king slips into madness and wanders about accompanied by his faithful Fool. He is aided by the Earl of Kent, who, though banished from the kingdom

HAMARTIA

The inherent defect or shortcoming in the hero of a tragedy, who is in other respects a superior being favoured by fortune, is called hamartia, or tragic flaw. The word *hamartia* is derived from the Greek hamartanein, meaning "to err."

Aristotle introduced the term casually in the *Poetics* in describing the tragic hero as a man of noble rank and nature whose misfortune is not brought about by villainy but by some "error of judgment" (hamartia). This imperfection later came to be interpreted as a moral flaw, such as Othello's jealousy or Hamlet's irresolution, although most great tragedies defy such a simple interpretation. Most importantly, the hero's suffering and its far-reaching reverberations are far out of proportion to his flaw. An element of cosmic collusion among the hero's flaw, chance, necessity, and other external forces is essential to bring about the tragic catastrophe.

In Greek tragedy the nature of the hero's flaw is even more elusive. Often the tragic deeds are committed unwittingly, as when Oedipus unknowingly kills his father and marries his own mother. If the deeds are committed knowingly, they are not committed by choice: Orestes is under obligation to Apollo to avenge his father's murder by killing his mother. Also, an apparent weakness is often only an excess of virtue, such as an extreme probity or zeal for perfection. It has been suggested in such cases, since the tragic hero is never passive but struggles to resolve his tragic difficulty with an obsessive dedication, that he is guilty of hubris—i.e., presumption of being godlike and attempting to overstep his human limitations.

for having supported Cordelia, has remained in Britain disguised as a loyal follower of the king. Cordelia, having married the king of France, is obliged to invade her

Image from a 2010 rehearsal of King Lear, *as performed by Australia's Bell Shakespeare Company, showing Cordelia (Susan Prior) and her maddened father Lear (John Bell).* Greg Wood/AFP/Getty Images

native country with a French army in order to rescue her neglected father. She is brought to Lear, cares for him, and helps him regain his reason. When her army is defeated, she and her father are taken into custody.

The subplot concerns the Earl of Gloucester, who gullibly believes the lies of his conniving illegitimate son, Edmund, and spurns his honest son, Edgar. Driven into exile disguised as a mad beggar, Edgar becomes a companion of the truly mad Lear and the Fool during a terrible storm. Edmund allies himself with Regan and Goneril to defend Britain against the French army mobilized by Cordelia. He turns his father over to Regan's brutal husband—the Duke of Cornwall, who gouges out Gloucester's eyes—and then imprisons Cordelia and Lear, but he is defeated in chivalric combat by Edgar. Jealous of Edmund's romantic attentions to Regan, Goneril poisons her and commits suicide. Cordelia is hanged on the orders of Edmund, who experiences a change of heart once he has been defeated and fatally wounded by Edgar but is too late in his attempt to reverse the death order. The Duke of Albany, Goneril's well-meaning husband, has attempted to remedy injustice in the kingdom but sees at last that events have overwhelmed his good intentions. Lear, broken, dies with Cordelia's body in his arms.

Daughters and fathers are at the heart of the major dilemma in *King Lear*. In this configuration, Shakespeare does what he often does in his late plays: erase the wife from the picture, so that father and daughter(s) are left to deal with one another. (Compare *Othello*, *The Winter's Tale*, *Cymbeline*, *The Tempest*, and perhaps the circumstances of Shakespeare's own life, in which his relationship to his daughter Susanna especially seems to have meant more to him than his partly estranged marriage with Anne.) Lear's banishing of Cordelia brings about his downfall. Concurrently, in the play's second plot, the Earl of Gloucester makes a similar mistake with his good-hearted son, Edgar, and thereby delivers himself into the hands of his scheming son, Edmund. Both these erring elderly fathers are ultimately nurtured by the loyal children they have banished, but not before the play has tested to its absolute limit the proposition that evil can flourish in a bad world.

The gods seem indifferent, perhaps absent entirely. Pleas to them for assistance go unheeded while the storm of fortune rains down on the heads of those who have trusted in conventional pieties. Part of what is so great in this play is that its testing of the major characters requires them to seek out philosophical answers that can arm the resolute heart against ingratitude and misfortune by

LEIR

The figure on whom Shakespeare based King Lear's aging monarch is derived from the 12th-century fictional history of Britain by Geoffrey of Monmouth. This book, *Historia regum Britanniae* (Latin: "History of the Kings of Britain"), published sometime between 1135 and 1139, was one of the most popular books of the Middle Ages. The story begins with the settlement of Britain by Brutus the Trojan, great-grandson of Aeneas, and by the Trojan Corineus, the eponymous founder of Cornwall, who exterminate giants inhabiting Britain. Then follow the reigns of the early kings down to the Roman conquest, including the founding of the city of Bath by Bladud and of Leicester by Leir (Lear), and the division of Leir's kingdom between the two ungrateful daughters. The story of the Saxon infiltration during the reign of the wicked usurper Vortigern, of the successful resistance of the Saxons by Vortimer, and of the restoration of the rightful line, followed by the great reigns of Aurelius and his brother Uther Pendragon, leads up to the account of King Arthur's conquests, the culminating point of the work.

Denounced from the first by sober historians, Geoffrey's fictional history nevertheless had an enormous influence on later chroniclers. Romanticized versions in the vernacular, the so-called *Bruts*, were in circulation from about 1150. Writers of the later Middle Ages gave the material a wide currency. Indeed Geoffrey's influence was at its peak after the accession of the Tudors.

constantly pointing out that life owes one nothing. The consolations of philosophy preciously found out by Edgar and Cordelia are those that rely not on the suppositious gods but on an inner moral strength demanding that one be charitable and honest because life is otherwise monstrous and subhuman. The play exacts terrible prices of those who persevere in goodness, but it leaves them and the reader, or audience, with the reassurance that it is simply better to be a Cordelia than to be a Goneril, to be an Edgar than to be an Edmund.

MACBETH

Shakespeare's tragedy *Macbeth* was written sometime in 1606–07 and published in the First Folio of 1623 from a playbook or a transcript of one. Some portions of the original text are corrupted or missing from the published edition. The play is the shortest of Shakespeare's tragedies, without diversions or subplots. It chronicles Macbeth's seizing of power and subsequent destruction, both his rise and his fall the result of blind ambition.

Macbeth and Banquo, who are generals serving King Duncan of Scotland, meet the Weird Sisters, three witches who prophesy that Macbeth will become thane of Cawdor, then king, and that Banquo will beget kings. Soon thereafter Macbeth discovers that he has indeed been made thane of Cawdor, which leads him to believe the rest of the prophecy. When King Duncan chooses this moment to honour Macbeth by visiting his castle of Dunsinane at Inverness, both Macbeth and his ambitious wife realize that the moment has arrived for them to carry out a plan of regicide that they have long contemplated. Spurred by his wife, Macbeth kills Duncan, and the murder is discovered when Macduff, the thane of Fife, arrives to call on the king. Duncan's sons Malcolm and Donalbain flee the country, fearing for their lives. Their speedy departure seems to implicate them in the crime, and Macbeth becomes king.

Worried by the witches' prophecy that Banquo's heirs instead of Macbeth's own progeny will be kings, Macbeth

The cover of the score to Guiseppi Verdi's opera Macbeth—based on Shakespeare's play—depicting Macbeth and Banquo's encounter with the three witches. Hulton Archive/Getty Images

arranges the death of Banquo, though Banquo's son Fleance escapes. Banquo's ghost haunts Macbeth, and Lady Macbeth is driven to madness by her guilt. The witches assure Macbeth that he will be safe until Birnam Wood comes to Dunsinane and that no one "of woman born" shall harm him. Learning that Macduff is joining Malcolm's army, Macbeth orders the slaughter of Macduff's wife and children. When the army, using branches from Birnam Wood as camouflage, advances on Dunsinane, Macbeth sees the prophecy being fulfilled: Birnam Wood has indeed come to Dunsinane. Lady Macbeth dies, and Macbeth is killed in battle by Macduff, who was "from his mother's womb untimely ripped" by cesarean section and in that quibbling sense was not "of woman born." Malcolm becomes the rightful king.

Macbeth is in some ways Shakespeare's most unsettling tragedy, because it invites the intense examination of the heart of a man who is well-intentioned in most ways but who discovers that he cannot resist the temptation to achieve power at any cost. Macbeth is a sensitive, even poetic person, and as such he understands with frightening clarity the stakes that are involved in his contemplated deed of murder. Duncan is a virtuous king and Macbeth's guest. The deed is regicide and murder and a violation of the sacred obligations of hospitality. Macbeth knows that Duncan's virtues, like angels, "trumpet-tongued," will plead against "the deep damnation of his taking-off" (Act I, scene 7, lines 19–20). The only factor weighing on the other side is personal ambition, which Macbeth understands to be a moral failing. The question of why he proceeds to murder is partly answered by the insidious temptations of the three Weird Sisters, who sense Macbeth's vulnerability to their prophecies, and the terrifying strength of his wife, who drives him on to the murder by describing his reluctance as unmanliness. Ultimately, though, the responsibility lies with Macbeth.

MACBETH THE MAN

The legend of the life of Macbeth, king of Scots (1040–57), was the basis of Shakespeare's *Macbeth*. He was probably a grandson of King Kenneth II (reigned 971–995), and he married Gruoch, a descendant of King Kenneth III (reigned 997–1005). About 1031 Macbeth succeeded his father, Findlaech (Sinel in Shakespeare), as mormaer, or chief, in the province of Moray, in northern Scotland. Macbeth established himself on the throne after killing his cousin King Duncan I in battle near Elgin—not, as in Shakespeare, by murdering Duncan in bed—on Aug. 14, 1040. Both Duncan and Macbeth derived their rights to the crown through their mothers.

MACBETH.

Portrait of the real-life King Macbeth. Hulton Archive/Getty Images

Macbeth's victory in 1045 over a rebel army, near Dunkeld (in the modern region of Perth and Kinross), may account for the later references (in Shakespeare and others) to Birnam Wood, for the village of Birnam is near Dunkeld. In 1046 Siward, earl of Northumbria, unsuccessfully attempted to dethrone Macbeth in favour of Malcolm (afterward King Malcolm III Canmore), eldest son of Duncan I. By 1050

Macbeth felt secure enough to leave Scotland for a pilgrimage to Rome. But in 1054 he was apparently forced by Siward to yield part of southern Scotland to Malcolm. Three years later Macbeth was killed in battle by Malcolm, with assistance from the English.

Macbeth was buried on the island of Iona, regarded as the resting place of lawful kings but not of usurpers. His followers installed his stepson, Lulach, as king. When Lulach was killed on March 17, 1058, Malcolm III was left supreme in Scotland.

ANTONY AND CLEOPATRA

Shakespeare's tragedy *Antony and Cleopatra* was written in 1606–07 and published in the First Folio of 1623 from an authorial draft in a more finished state than most of his working papers or possibly from a transcript of those papers not yet prepared as a playbook. It is considered one of Shakespeare's richest and most moving works. The principal source of the play was Sir Thomas North's *Parallel Lives* (1579), an English version of Plutarch's *Bioi paralléloi.*

The story concerns Mark Antony, Roman military leader and triumvir, who is besottedly in love with Cleopatra, queen of Egypt and former mistress of Pompey and Julius Caesar. Summoned to Rome upon the death of his wife, Fulvia, who had openly antagonized his fellow triumvir Octavius, Antony heals the residual political rift by marrying Octavius's sister, Octavia. Word of the event enrages Cleopatra. Renewed contention with Octavius and desire for Cleopatra, however, send Antony back to his lover's arms. When the rivalry erupts into warfare, Cleopatra accompanies Antony to the Battle of Actium, where her presence proves militarily disastrous. She heads back to Egypt, and Antony follows, pursued by Octavius. Anticipating the eventual outcome, Antony's friend and loyal officer Enobarbus deserts him and joins Octavius. At Alexandria, Octavius eventually defeats Antony. Cleopatra, fearing for her life in light of Antony's increasingly erratic behaviour, sends a false report of her suicide, which prompts Antony to wound himself mortally. Carried by his soldiers to the queen's hiding place in one of her monuments, he dies in her arms. Rather than submit to Roman conquest, the grieving Cleopatra arranges to have a poisonous snake delivered to her in a basket of figs. Attended by her faithful servants Charmian and Iras, she kills herself.

Antony and Cleopatra approaches human frailty in terms that are less spiritually terrifying. The story of the lovers is certainly one of worldly failure. Plutarch's *Lives* gave to Shakespeare the object lesson of a brave general who lost his reputation and sense of self-worth through his infatuation with an admittedly attractive but nonetheless dangerous woman. Shakespeare changes none of the circumstances: Antony hates himself for dallying in Egypt with Cleopatra, agrees to marry with Octavius Caesar's sister Octavia as a way of recovering his status in the Roman triumvirate, cheats on Octavia eventually, loses the Battle of Actium because of his fatal attraction for Cleopatra, and dies in Egypt a defeated, aging warrior. Shakespeare adds to this narrative a compelling portrait of midlife crisis. Antony is deeply anxious about his loss of sexual potency and position in the world of affairs. His amorous life in Egypt is manifestly an attempt to affirm and recover his dwindling male power.

Yet the Roman model is not in Shakespeare's play the unassailably virtuous choice that it is in Plutarch. In *Antony*

CLEOPATRA THROUGH THE AGES

The historical Egyptian queen Cleopatra is famous as the lover of Julius Caesar and later the wife of Mark Antony. She became queen on the death of her father, Ptolemy XII, in 51 BCE and ruled successively with her two brothers Ptolemy XIII (51–47) and Ptolemy XIV (47–44) and her son Ptolemy XV Caesar (44–30). After the Roman armies of Octavian (the future emperor Augustus) defeated their combined forces, Antony and Cleopatra committed suicide, and Egypt fell under Roman domination.

The vast majority of Egypt's many hundreds of queens, although famed throughout their own land, were more or less unknown in the outside world. As the dynastic age ended and the hieroglyphic script was lost, the queens' stories were forgotten and their monuments buried under Egypt's sands. But Cleopatra had lived in a highly literate age, and her actions had influenced the formation of the Roman Empire. Her story could not be forgotten. Octavian (the future emperor Augustus) published his own autobiography and censored Rome's official records. As Cleopatra had played a key role in his struggle to power, her story was preserved as an integral part of his. But it was diminished to just two episodes: her relationships with Julius Caesar and Mark Antony. Cleopatra, stripped of any political validity, was to be seen as the prototype of the romantic femme fatale.

This official Roman version of a predatory, immoral Cleopatra passed into Western culture, where it was retold and reinterpreted as the years passed, until it evolved into a story of a wicked life made good by an honourable death. Meanwhile, Muslim scholars, writing after the Arab conquest of Egypt about 640 CE, developed their own version of the queen. Their Cleopatra was first and foremost a scholar and a scientist, a gifted philosopher and a chemist.

Shakespeare's Cleopatra is more sympathetic than Plutarch's and his queen is a true heroine. His was by no means the first revision of Cleopatra, nor was it to be the last, but his is the Cleopatra that has lingered longest in the public imagination.

and Cleopatra Roman behaviour does promote attentiveness to duty and worldly achievement, but, as embodied in young Octavius, it is also obsessively male and cynical about women. Octavius is intent on capturing Cleopatra and leading her in triumph back to Rome — that is, to cage the unruly woman and place her under male control. When Cleopatra perceives that aim, she chooses a noble suicide rather than humiliation by a patriarchal male. In her suicide, Cleopatra avers that she has called "great Caesar ass / Unpolicied" (Act V, scene 2, lines 307–308). Vastly to be preferred is the fleeting dream of greatness with Antony, both of them unfettered, godlike, like Isis and Osiris, immortalized as heroic lovers even if the actual circumstances of their lives were often disappointing and even tawdry. The vision in this tragedy is deliberately unstable, but at its most ethereal it encourages a vision of human greatness that is distant from the soul-corrupting evil of Macbeth or King Lear.

OTHER TRAGEDIES

Two late tragedies, *Timon of Athens* and *Coriolanus*, also choose the ancient Classical world as their setting but do so in a deeply dispiriting way. Shakespeare appears to have been much preoccupied with ingratitude and human greed in these years.

TIMON OF ATHENS

Shakespeare's tragedy *Timon of Athens* was probably written sometime in 1605–08 and published in the First Folio of 1623 from an authorial manuscript, probably unfinished. Some parts of the play may be by Thomas Middleton. It belongs to Shakespeare's late experimental period, when he explored a new kind of tragic form.

Unlike the plots of his great tragedies, the story of *Timon of Athens* is simple and lacks development. It demonstrates events in the life of Timon, a man known for his great and universal generosity, who spends his fortune and then is spurned when he requires help. He puts on a feast, invites his fair-weather friends, serves them warm water, and throws it in their faces. Leaving Athens filled with hatred, he goes to live in a cave. There he is visited by his loyal servant Flavius, by the churlish philosopher Apemantus, and by two mistresses of the general Alcibiades, all of whom sympathize to some degree with Timon's plight, but to no avail. Timon has turned his back on ungrateful humankind. While digging for roots to eat, Timon uncovers gold, most of which he gives to Alcibiades' mistresses and to Alcibiades himself for his war against Athens. Word of his fortune reaches Athens, and, as a variety of Athenians importune Timon again, he curses them and dies.

Timon of Athens may never have been produced. The unrelieved bitterness of this account is only partly ameliorated by the story of the military captain Alcibiades, who also has been the subject of Athenian ingratitude and forgetfulness but who manages to reassert his authority at the end. Alcibiades resolves to make some accommodation with the wretched condition of humanity, though Timon will have none of it.

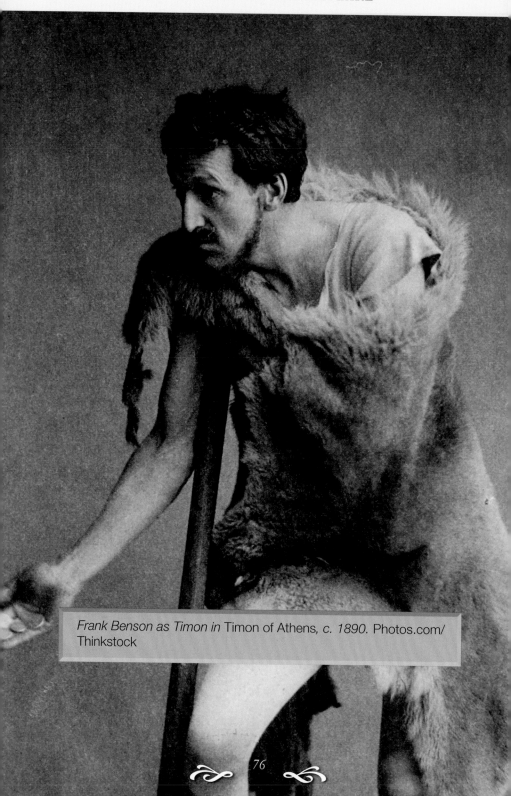

Frank Benson as Timon in Timon of Athens, *c. 1890.* Photos.com/ Thinkstock

CORIOLANUS

The last of Shakespeare's so-called political tragedies, *Coriolanus*, was written about 1608 and published in the First Folio of 1623 seemingly from the playbook, which had preserved some features of the authorial manuscript. Based on the life of Gnaeus Marcius Coriolanus, a legendary Roman hero of the late 6th and early 5th centuries BCE, it is essentially an expansion of the Plutarchan biography in *Parallel Lives*. Though it is Elizabethan in structure, it is markedly Classical in tone.

The action of the play follows Caius Marcius (afterward Caius Marcius Coriolanus) through several phases of his career. He is shown as an arrogant young nobleman in peacetime, as a bloodstained and valiant warrior against the city of Corioli, as a modest victor, and as a reluctant candidate for consul. When he refuses to flatter the Roman citizens, for whom he feels contempt, or to show them his wounds to win their vote, they turn on him and banish him. Bitterly he joins forces with his enemy Aufidius, a Volscian, against Rome. Leading the enemy to the edge of the city, Coriolanus is ultimately persuaded by his mother, Volumnia—who brings with her Coriolanus's wife, Virgilia, and his son—to make peace with Rome, and in the end he is killed at the instigation of his Volscian ally.

Coriolanus is in many ways unusual for Shakespearean drama. It has a single narrative line, its images are compact and striking, and its most effective moments are characterized by understatement or silence. When the banished Coriolanus returns at the head of the opposing army, he says little to Menenius, the trusted family friend and politician, or to Volumnia, both of whom have come to plead for Rome. His mother's argument is long and sustained, and for more than 50 lines he listens, until his resolution is broken from within. Then, as a stage direction in the original edition

A scene from William Shakespeare's Coriolanus, *undated engraving.*
Library of Congress, Washington, D.C.

testifies, he "holds her by the hand, silent." In his own words, he has "obey[ed] instinct" and betrayed his dependence. He cannot "stand / As if a man were author of himself / And knew no other kin." Thus is his desire for revenge defeated. While his mother is hailed as "patroness, the life of Rome," Coriolanus stands accused of treachery by Aufidius and is cut down by Aufidius's supporters.

Like *Timon of Athens*, *Coriolanus* portrays the ungrateful responses of a city toward its military hero. The problem is complicated by the fact that Coriolanus, egged on by his mother and his conservative allies, undertakes a political role in Rome for which he is not temperamentally fitted. His friends urge him to hold off his intemperate speech until he is voted into office, but Coriolanus is too plainspoken to be tactful in this way. His contempt for the plebeians and their political leaders, the tribunes, is unsparing. His political philosophy, while relentlessly aristocratic and snobbish, is consistent and theoretically sophisticated. The citizens are, as he argues, incapable of governing themselves judiciously. Yet his own unwillingness to govern himself only makes matters worse. As a tragedy, *Coriolanus* is again bitter, satirical, ending in defeat and humiliation. It is an immensely powerful play, and it captures a philosophical mood of nihilism and bitterness that hovers over Shakespeare's writings throughout these years in the first decade of the 1600s.

TROILUS AND CRESSIDA

Three of Shakespeare's plays—*Troilus and Cressida*, *All's Well That Ends Well*, and *Measure for Measure*—are hard to classify in terms of genre. Thus all three are sometimes grouped today as "problem" plays. *Troilus and Cressida* is the most experimental and puzzling of these three.

Shakespeare's *Troilus and Cressida* was written about 1601–02 and printed in a quarto edition in two different "states" in 1609, probably from the author's working draft. The editors of the First Folio of 1623 may have had copyright difficulties in obtaining permission to include this play in their collection. Based on George Chapman's translation of the *Iliad* and on 15th-century accounts of the Trojan War by John Lydgate and William Caxton, *Troilus and Cressida* is an often cynical exploration of the causes of strife between and within the Greek and Trojan armies—the betrayal of love, the absence of heroism, and the emptiness of honour. The play was also influenced by Geoffrey Chaucer's love poem *Troilus and Criseyde*, although Shakespeare's treatment of the lovers and his attitude toward their dilemma is in sharp contrast to Chaucer's.

Troilus and Cressida *(Act V, scene 2), engraving by Luigi Schiavonetti, after a painting by Angelica Kauffmann, c. 1795.* Popular Graphic Arts/Library of Congress, Washington, D.C. (neg. no. LC-DIG-pga-03274)

Cressida, a Trojan woman whose father has defected to the Greeks, pledges her love to Troilus, one of King Priam's sons. However, when her father demands her presence in the Greek camp, she reluctantly accepts the attentions of Diomedes, the Greek officer who has been sent to escort her to the Greek side. Given her situation in an enemy camp and being an attractive woman among sex-starved warriors, she has few choices. The love between Troilus and Cressida, begun on such a hopeful note, is at last overwhelmed by the circumstances of war that they cannot control. Meanwhile, the war itself is presented in all its seamy aspects, since it is at bottom a senseless war fought over the possession of Helen, wife of Menelaus of Sparta but now the mistress of the Trojan prince Paris. Their one scene together presents Helen and Paris as vapid and self-centred.

Other figures fare no less well. The legendary Greek hero Achilles is depicted as petulant and greedy for honour, so much so that he brutally massacres the great Hector when that warrior is unarmed. Hector, for his part, is at once the wisest of the Trojans and a captive of his own sense of honour that obliges him to go into battle when his wife and family all warn him of ominous prognostications. The Greek general Agamemnon is given to long-winded speeches, as is old Nestor. Ulysses, the most astute of the Greek generals, is right-minded about many things but also cynical and calculating. Ajax, another Greek officer, is an oaf, easily put upon by his colleagues. Thersites, a deformed Greek, comments wryly on the actions of the other characters, while Pandarus, the bawdy go-between of the lovers, enjoys watching their degradation. The drama ends on a note of complete moral and political disintegration.

It is easy to see how *Troilus and Cressida* defies genre identification. It can hardly be a comedy, ending as it does in the deaths of Patroclus and Hector and the looming defeat of the Trojans. Nor is the ending normative in terms of romantic comedy since the lovers, Troilus and Cressida, are separated from one another and embittered by the failure of their relationship. The play is a history play in a sense, because it deals with the great Trojan War celebrated in Homer's *Iliad*. And yet its purpose is hardly that of telling the story of the war. As a tragedy, it is perplexing in that the chief figures of the play (apart from Hector) do not die at the end, and the mood is one of desolation and even disgust rather than tragic catharsis.

Perhaps the play should be thought of as a satire. The choric observations of Thersites and Pandarus serve throughout as a mordant commentary on the interconnectedness of war and lechery. With fitting ambiguity, the play was placed in the Folio of 1623 between the histories and the tragedies, in a category all by itself.

Conclusion

S hakespeare wrote tragedies (and near-tragedies) throughout his career, from his apprenticeship to his full maturity. Whatever the main thrust of these works, be it revenge, jealousy, blind ambition, foolish pride, or some other all-too-human motivation, Shakespeare was able to examine it deeply and from many angles. Whoever the plays' main characters (young lovers, aging generals, storied queens), Shakespeare was able to present them as richly three-dimensional individuals with complex feelings and perceptions, and he makes us identify with them and feel what they feel. His genius lies in that gift. The language of the age, though it is sometimes difficult to understand, amply rewards the persistent reader or playgoer with its aptness and beauty. Rare is the playgoer, even in the 21st century, who can leave the performance of a Shakespearean tragedy unmoved or unschooled in some way. There is no doubt whatsoever that Shakespeare's lessons remain significant and universal today, some four centuries after his death.

abjure The act of abstaining from or completely rejecting something or someone.

allegory A symbolic fictional narrative that conveys a meaning not explicitly set forth in the narrative, such as a fable or parable.

animus An attitude marked by prejudice, often spiteful or filled with ill will.

anomaly A deviation from normal.

bombastic Marked by pretentious language.

enclosure The division of communal farmland into individually owned and managed plots.

geopolitical Marked by a combination of political and geographic factors.

guild An association of people with similar interests or pursuits.

iconoclastic Relating to an attack on another's beliefs, particularly religious beliefs.

interstitial Situated in the spaces between something that is generally continuous.

liberties Areas of populated land located on the outskirts of a city.

masque A dramatic verse composition usually performed by masked actors that represent mythological or allegorical figures.

melodrama A work, such as a play, that is characterized by excessive theatricality, concentrating on plot and physical action over characterization.

mise-en-scène The physical setting of a play; also, the arrangement of actors and scenery on a stage.

palinode An ode, song, or poem recanting or retracting something written in an earlier poem.

quarto A book printed on paper cut four to a sheet.

rhetoric The art of writing or speaking as a means of communication or persuasion.

secularization The act of transferring a possession or control from ecclesiastical to civil or lay use, possession, or control.

shrew A negative term used to describe a woman who has a bad temper and is disagreeable.

tableaux In the theatre, a depiction of a scene usually presented on a stage by silent and motionless costumed participants.

tinker One who fixes or mends household items.

transmutation The conversion of one element into another, either by natural or artificial means.

vagabond A person who wanders idly from place to place.

Bibliography

Modern editions of Shakespeare's works include Stanley Wells and Gary Taylor (eds.), *William Shakespeare, The Complete Works,* 2nd ed. (2005); G. Blakemore Evans and J.J. Tobin (eds.), *The Riverside Shakespeare,* 2nd ed. (1998); David Bevington (ed.), *The Complete Works of Shakespeare,* 6th ed. (2009); and Stephen Greenblatt (ed.), *The Norton Shakespeare,* 2nd ed. (2008).

Studies of the history of the Elizabethan playhouse and acting companies include Glynne Wickham, *Early English Stages, 1300 to 1660,* 3 vol. in 4 (1959–81); and Andrew Gurr, *The Shakespearean Stage, 1574–1642,* 4th ed. (2009); the latter is a thorough and concise overview and reflects recent historical and archaeological findings. William Ingram, *The Business of Playing: The Beginnings of the Adult Professional Theater in Elizabethan London* (1992), offers a detailed account of pre-Shakespearean acting companies.

Many aspects of Elizabethan life and culture are cogently presented in Russ McDonald, *The Bedford Companion to Shakespeare,* 2nd ed. (2001), which also includes well-selected documents from the period. A more detailed account of the significance of the liberties and playhouses is found in Steven Mullaney, *The Place of the Stage: License, Play, and Power in Renaissance England* (1988, reissued 1995). Studies that represent New Historical approaches to Elizabethan culture and drama—in which the works of Shakespeare and others are set firmly in their historical context—are Stephen Greenblatt, *Renaissance Self-Fashioning: From More to Shakespeare* (1980), *Shakespearean Negotiations: The Circulation of Social Energy in Renaissance England* (1988), and *Will in the World: How Shakespeare Became Shakespeare* (2004); and Louis Montrose, *The Purpose of Playing: Shakespeare and the Cultural Politics of the Elizabethan Theatre* (1996). Jean-Christophe Agnew, *Worlds Apart: The Market and the Theater in Anglo-American Thought, 1550–1750* (1986), provides a valuable study of early modern theatre and emerging market economies. An influential materialist-feminist study of the stage is Jean E. Howard, *The Stage and Social Struggle in Early Modern England* (1994), which includes her previously published and often-cited work on cross-dressing. Janet Adelman, *Suffocating Mothers: Fantasies of Maternal Origin in Shakespeare's Plays, Hamlet to The Tempest* (1992), combines feminism and psychoanalytic theory in a compelling argument about selected plays. Stephen Orgel, *Impersonations: The Performance of Gender in Shakespeare's England* (1996), provides a seminal study of gender, sexuality, and cross-dressing (both onstage and off).

Other works addressing Shakespeare and tragedy are A.C. Bradley, *Shakespearean Tragedy,* 3rd ed. (1992); Arthur Kirsch, *The Passions of Shakespeare's Tragic Heroes* (1990); and Maynard Mack, *King Lear in Our Time* (1965), and *Everybody's Shakespeare: Reflections Chiefly on the Tragedies* (1993); and Philippa Berry, *Shakespeare's Feminine Endings: Disfiguring Death in the Tragedies* (1999).

Index

A

actors, view of, 12–14
Antony and Cleopatra, 34, 39, 40, 44, 54, 55, 71–74

B

bearbaiting, 5, 7, 8
boys' companies, 10, 12
Brayne, John, 1
Burbage, Cuthbert, 4–5
Burbage, James, 1, 3
Burbage, Richard, 4–5

C

Chamberlain's Men, 1, 3, 5, 21, 48, 56
Chaucer, Geoffrey, 20, 26, 79–80
Christian tragedy, 30–34
Cleopatra, about, 73–74
Coriolanus, 74, 77–79

D

Doctor Faustus, 30, 33–34
domestic tragedy, 44
drama, as genre, 10–11, 14–16

E

Elizabeth I, 6, 7, 31, 32, 41
Elizabethan tragedy, 27–30

F

Fates, the, 37, 38
First Folio, 46, 50, 52, 56, 60, 62, 67, 71, 75, 77, 79, 82

G

Globe Theatre, the, 1–2, 4–5, 17

H

hamartia, 61, 63
Hamlet, 34, 37, 39, 41, 44, 45, 48, 54–59, 63
internal play in, 21–23, 25
Henry V, 21, 25
heroic tragedy, 44

J

James I, 10, 41
Jonson, Ben, 35
Julius Caesar, 44, 52–54

K

King Lear, 34, 37, 39, 41, 44, 54, 55, 62–67, 74
Kyd, Thomas, 45, 48–49, 56

L

"liberties" of London, 1, 6–10, 16
London
    city playhouses, 10–12, 14

"liberties" of, 1, 6–10, 16
the popular stage in, 14–16
and view of actors, 12–14
Love's Labour's Lost, 18

M

Macbeth, 34, 37, 39, 40, 41, 44, 54, 55, 67–69, 74
Macbeth, about, 70–71
Marlowe, Christopher, 30–34, 40, 41, 48, 49
Midsummer Night's Dream, A, 18
internal play in, 19–20
Milton, John, 43
Murder of Gonzago, The, 21–23, 25

O

Oedipus, 34, 37, 39, 63
Othello, 34, 37, 44, 54, 55, 59–62, 63, 65

P

playhouses, city, 10–12, 14
political tragedy, 44
Puritans, 5, 10, 12, 13–14, 41
Pyramus and Thisbe, 19–20, 25

R

revenge tragedy, 44, 45, 48, 49, 58
Romeo and Juliet, 20, 44, 50–52

S

Shakespeare, William
from comedy to tragedy, 35–37
and Globe Theatre, 5

performance in Shakespeare's theatre, 17–25
and plays within plays, 18–19
and theatre in London, 1, 5
tragedies of, 34–35, 39–40, 44–82
tragic art of, 39–40, 83
social tragedy, 44
Spanish Tragedy, The, 45, 48, 49

T

Tamburlaine, 30, 32–33, 34
Taming of the Shrew, The, 18–19
Tempest, The, 40, 65
internal play in, 23–25
theatre, during Shakespeare's time, 1–6, 8, 10–16, 41
performance in, 17–25
Theatre, The, 1–2, 4, 5
Timon of Athens, 74–77, 78
Titus Andronicus, 44, 45, 46–49, 58
tragedy, in Shakespeare's time, 26–43
Christian, 30–34
decline of in 17th-century England, 41–43
Elizabethan, 27–30
Shakespearean, 34–35, 44–82
transvestite actors, 12–14
Troilus and Cressida, 79–82

W

Webster, John, 41, 42–43
West Side Story, 51–52